Let's Keep in Touch

Follow Us

Visit US at

www.EffortlessMath.com

Call

1-469-230-3605

Online

 https://www.facebook.com/Effortlessmath

 https://goo.gl/2B6qWW

Online Math Lessons

It's easy! Here's how it works.

1- Request a FREE introductory session.

2- Meet a Math tutor online.

3- Start Learning Math in Minutes.

Send Email to: info@EffortlessMath.com

Or Call: +1-469-230-3605

Grade 6 STAAR Mathematics Workbook 2018 – 2019

A Comprehensive Review and Step–by–Step Guide to Preparing for the STAAR Math Test

By

Reza Nazari

& Ava Ross

All inquiries should be addressed to:

info@effortlessMath.com

www.EffortlessMath.com

ISBN-13: 978-1987665796

ISBN-10: 1987665791

Published by: Effortless Math Education

www.EffortlessMath.com

Description

Grade 6 STAAR Mathematics Workbook is full of specific and detailed material that will be key to succeeding on the STAAR Math. It's filled with the critical math concepts a student will need in order to do well on the test. Math concepts in this book break down the topics, so the material can be quickly grasped. Examples are worked step–by–step, so you learn exactly what to do.

This comprehensive Math workbook brings together everything a student needs to know for the STAAR Math section. It is designed to address the needs of STAAR test takers who must have a working knowledge of basic Math. It contains most common sample questions that are most likely to appear in the mathematics section of the STAAR. This book leaves no stones unturned!

STAAR Mathematics Workbook with over 2,500 sample questions and 2 complete STAAR tests is all a student needs to fully prepare for the STAAR Math. It will help the student learns everything they need to ace the math section of the STAAR.

This workbook includes practice test questions. It contains easy–to–read essential summaries that highlight the key areas of the STAAR Math test. Effortless Math test study guide reviews the most important components of the STAAR Math test. Anyone planning to take the STAAR Math test should take advantage of the review material and practice test questions contained in this study guide.

Inside the pages of this comprehensive book, students can learn basic math operations in a structured manner with a complete study program to help them understand essential math skills. It also has many exciting features, including:

- Dynamic design and easy–to–follow activities
- Step–by–step guide for all Math topics
- Targeted, skill–building practices
- A fun, interactive and concrete learning process
- Math topics are grouped by category, so you can focus on the topics you struggle on
- All solutions for the exercises are included, so you will always find the answers
- 2 Complete STAAR Math Practice Tests that reflect the format and question types on STAAR

STAAR Mathematics Workbook is the ideal prep solution for any student who wants to prepare for the STAAR test. It efficiently and effectively reinforces learning outcomes through engaging questions and repeated practice, helping students to quickly master basic Math skills.

Effortless Math books have helped thousands of students prepare for standardized tests and achieve their education and career goals. This is done by setting high standards and preparing the best quality Mathematics learning books, and this book is no exception. It is the perfect study aid for the STAAR Math test. The student will definitely be well prepared for the test with this comprehensive workbook!

About the Author

Reza Nazari is the author of more than 100 Math learning books including:
− **Math and Critical Thinking Challenges:** For the Middle and High School Student
− **GED Math in 30 Days.**
− **ASVAB Math Workbook 2018 - 2019**
− **Effortless Math Education Workbooks**
− **and many more Mathematics books ...**

Reza is also an experienced Math instructor and a test−prep expert who has been tutoring students since 2008. Reza is the founder of Effortless Math Education, a tutoring company that has helped many students raise their standardized test scores—and attend the colleges of their dreams. Reza provides an individualized custom learning plan and the personalized attention that makes a difference in how students view math.

To ask questions about Math, you can contact Reza via email at:
reza@EffortlessMath.com

Find Reza's professional profile at:
goo.gl/zoC9rJ

Contents

Chapter 1: Whole Number Operations

1–1 Adding Whole Numbers

1–2 Subtracting Whole Numbers

1–3 Dividing Whole Numbers

1–4 Multiplying Whole Numbers

1–5 Rounding whole numbers

1–6 Whole number estimation

1–1 Adding Whole Numbers

Helpful

Hints

1– Line up the numbers.
2– Start with the unit place. (ones place)
3– Regroup if necessary.
4– Add the tens place.
5– Continue with other digits.

Example:

$$1,349$$
$$+2,411$$
$$\overline{3,760}$$

Add.

1)
$$\begin{array}{r} 1,158 \\ +\ 6,687 \\ \hline \end{array}$$

3)
$$\begin{array}{r} 5,756 \\ +\ 2,712 \\ \hline \end{array}$$

5)
$$\begin{array}{r} 4,257 \\ +5,194 \\ \hline \end{array}$$

2)
$$\begin{array}{r} 5,188 \\ +\ 1,298 \\ \hline \end{array}$$

4)
$$\begin{array}{r} 3,239 \\ +2,562 \\ \hline \end{array}$$

6)
$$\begin{array}{r} 6,215 \\ +2,189 \\ \hline \end{array}$$

Find the missing numbers.

7) 1145 + ___ = 1276

8) 500 + 1000 = ___

9) 3200 + ___ = 4300

10) 455 + ___ = 1755

11) ___ + 720 = 1250

12) ___ + 670 = 2230

13) David sells gems. He finds a diamond in Istanbul and buys it for $3,433. Then, he flies to Cairo and purchases a bigger diamond for the bargain price of $5,922. How much does David spend on the two diamonds? _____

1–2 Subtracting Whole Numbers

Helpful

Hints

1– Line up the numbers.
2– Start with the units place. (ones place)
3– Regroup if necessary.
4– Subtract the tens place.
5– Continue with other digits.

Example:

$$\begin{array}{r} 5,397 \\ -\ 2,416 \\ \hline 2,981 \end{array}$$

Subtract.

1)
$$\begin{array}{r} 8,519 \\ -\ 5,422 \\ \hline \end{array}$$

3)
$$\begin{array}{r} 7,821 \\ -\ 3,212 \\ \hline \end{array}$$

5)
$$\begin{array}{r} 9,290 \\ -\ 3,829 \\ \hline \end{array}$$

2)
$$\begin{array}{r} 6,222 \\ -\ 4,331 \\ \hline \end{array}$$

4)
$$\begin{array}{r} 8,756 \\ -\ 6,712 \\ \hline \end{array}$$

6)
$$\begin{array}{r} 5,117 \\ -4,216 \\ \hline \end{array}$$

Find the missing number.

7) 2223 – ___ = 1120

10) 2300 – ___ = 1250

8) 3574 – ___ = 2245

11) 3780 – 1890 = ___

9) 1124 – 578 = ___

12) 2880 – 2560 = ___

13) Jackson had \$3,963 invested in the stock market until he lost \$2,171 on those investments. How much money does he have in the stock market now?

1–3 Dividing Whole Numbers

Helpful   – A typical division problem: **Example:**
                      Dividend ÷ Divisor = Quotient   18,000 ÷ 90 = 200

Hints   – In division, we want to find how many
                  times a number (divisor) is contained in
                  another number (dividend).
                  – The result in a division problem is the
                  quotient.

Find answers.

1) 500 ÷ 100

2) 4000 ÷ 400

3) 1, 500 ÷ 500

4) 1, 800 ÷ 300

5) 2, 700 ÷ 900

6) 800 ÷ 200

7) 1, 400 ÷ 200

8) 2, 500 ÷ 500

9) 4, 800 ÷ 600

10) 9000 ÷ 200

11) 3, 600 ÷ 600

12) 3, 000 ÷ 500

13) 1000 ÷ 200

14) 4, 500 ÷ 900

15) 1, 200 ÷ 600

16) 6, 000 ÷ 200

17) 9, 000 ÷ 300

18) 2, 800 ÷ 400

1–4 Multiplying Whole Numbers

Helpful

Hints

– Learn the times tables first!
– For multiplication, line up the numbers you are multiplying.
– Start with the ones place.
– Continue with other digits

Example:

$200 \times 90 = 18{,}000$

Find the answers.

1)
$$\begin{array}{r} 2400 \\ \times\ 13 \\ \hline \end{array}$$

5)
$$\begin{array}{r} 2500 \\ \times\ 5 \\ \hline \end{array}$$

9)
$$\begin{array}{r} 3191 \\ \times\ 78 \\ \hline \end{array}$$

2)
$$\begin{array}{r} 1200 \\ \times\ 10 \\ \hline \end{array}$$

6)
$$\begin{array}{r} 3200 \\ \times\ 25 \\ \hline \end{array}$$

10)
$$\begin{array}{r} 4200 \\ \times\ 12 \\ \hline \end{array}$$

3)
$$\begin{array}{r} 3120 \\ \times\ 9 \\ \hline \end{array}$$

7)
$$\begin{array}{r} 4178 \\ \times\ 34 \\ \hline \end{array}$$

11)
$$\begin{array}{r} 6800 \\ \times\ 10 \\ \hline \end{array}$$

4)
$$\begin{array}{r} 4000 \\ \times\ 4 \\ \hline \end{array}$$

8)
$$\begin{array}{r} 9256 \\ \times\ 26 \\ \hline \end{array}$$

12)
$$\begin{array}{r} 8000 \\ \times\ 55 \\ \hline \end{array}$$

1–5 Rounding Whole Numbers

Helpful

Hints

– Rounding is putting a number up or down to the nearest whole number or the nearest hundred, etc.

Example:
64 rounded to the nearest ten is 60, because 64 is closer to 60 than to 70.

Round each number to the underlined place value.

1) 19<u>7</u>2

2) 2,<u>9</u>95

3) 33<u>6</u>4

4) 12<u>8</u>1

5) 23<u>5</u>5

6) 13<u>3</u>4

7) 1,<u>2</u>03

8) 14<u>5</u>7

9) 7<u>4</u>84

10) 19<u>1</u>4

11) 42<u>3</u>9

12) <u>9</u>,123

13) 3,4<u>5</u>2

14) 2<u>5</u>69

15) 1,<u>2</u>30

16) 7<u>6</u>98

17) 92<u>9</u>3

18) 52<u>3</u>7

19) 24<u>9</u>3

20) 2,<u>9</u>23

21) <u>9</u>,845

22) 45<u>5</u>5

23) 6<u>9</u>39

24) 98<u>6</u>9

1–6 Whole Number Estimation

Helpful

Hints

– To estimate means to make a rough guess or calculation.
– To round means to simplify a number by scaling it slightly up or down.

Example:

$73 + 69 \approx 140$

Estimate the sum by rounding each added to the nearest ten.

1) $582 + 277$

2) $2771 + 1651$

3) $7436 + 3575$

4) $1542 + 8738$

5) $3843 + 6579$

6) $4722 + 8186$

7) $2419 + 7224$

8) $6768 + 3169$

9)
$$\begin{array}{r} 4{,}694 \\ + 7{,}359 \\ \hline \end{array}$$

10)
$$\begin{array}{r} 9{,}622 \\ + 6{,}114 \\ \hline \end{array}$$

11)
$$\begin{array}{r} 1{,}278 \\ + 5{,}313 \\ \hline \end{array}$$

12)
$$\begin{array}{r} 8{,}259 \\ + 7{,}229 \\ \hline \end{array}$$

Answers of Worksheets – Chapter 1

1–1 Adding Whole Numbers

1) 7,845	6) 8,404	11) 530
2) 6,486	7) 131	12) 1,560
3) 8,468	8) 1500	13) $9,355
4) 5,801	9) 1,100	
5) 9,451	10) 1300	

1–2 Subtracting Whole Numbers

1) 3,097	6) 901	11) 1,890
2) 1,891	7) 1,103	12) 320
3) 4,609	8) 1,329	13) 1,792
4) 2,044	9) 546	
5) 5,461	10) 1,050	

1–3 Dividing Whole Numbers

1) 5	7) 7	13) 5
2) 10	8) 5	14) 5
3) 3	9) 8	15) 2
4) 6	10) 45	16) 30
5) 3	11) 6	17) 30
6) 4	12) 6	18) 7

1–4 Multiplying Whole Numbers

1) 31,200	5) 12,500	9) 248,898
2) 12,000	6) 80,000	10) 50,400
3) 28,080	7) 142,052	11) 68,000
4) 16,000	8) 240,656	12) 440,000

1–5 Rounding whole numbers

1) 2000
2) 3000
3) 3360
4) 1280
5) 2360
6) 1330
7) 1200
8) 1460

9) 7500
10) 1910
11) 4240
12) 9000
13) 3450
14) 2600
15) 1200
16) 7700

17) 9290
18) 5240
19) 2490
20) 2900
21) 10,000
22) 4560
23) 6900
24) 9870

1–6 Whole number estimation

1) 860
2) 4420
3) 11020
4) 10280

5) 10420
6) 12910
7) 9640
8) 9940

9) 12050
10) 15730
11) 6590
12) 15490

Chapter 2: Arithmetic and Number Theory

2–1 Simplifying Fractions

2–2 Adding and Subtracting Fractions

2–3 Multiplying and Dividing Fractions

2–4 Adding and Subtracting Mixed Numbers

2–5 Multiplying and Dividing Mixed Numbers

2–6 Adding and Subtracting Decimals

2–7 Multiplying and Dividing Decimals

2–8 Converting Between Fractions, Decimals and Mixed Numbers

2–9 Rounding Numbers

2–10 Factoring Numbers

2–11 Prime Factorization

2–12 Greatest Common Factor

2–13 Least Common Multiple

2–14 Divisibility Rules

2–1 Simplifying Fractions

Helpful

Hints

- Evenly divide both the top and bottom of the fraction by 2, 3, 5, 7, ... etc.
- Continue until you can't go any further.

Example:

$$\frac{4}{12} = \frac{2}{6} = \frac{1}{3}$$

Simplify the fractions.

1) $\dfrac{22}{36}$

2) $\dfrac{8}{10}$

3) $\dfrac{12}{18}$

4) $\dfrac{6}{8}$

5) $\dfrac{13}{39}$

6) $\dfrac{5}{20}$

7) $\dfrac{16}{36}$

8) $\dfrac{18}{36}$

9) $\dfrac{20}{50}$

10) $\dfrac{6}{54}$

11) $\dfrac{45}{81}$

12) $\dfrac{21}{28}$

13) $\dfrac{35}{56}$

14) $\dfrac{52}{64}$

15) $\dfrac{13}{65}$

16) $\dfrac{44}{77}$

17) $\dfrac{21}{42}$

18) $\dfrac{15}{36}$

19) $\dfrac{9}{24}$

20) $\dfrac{20}{80}$

21) $\dfrac{25}{45}$

2–2 Adding and Subtracting Fractions

Helpful

Hints

- For "like" fractions (fractions with the same denominator), add or subtract the numerators and write the answer over the common denominator.
- Find equivalent fractions with the same denominator before you can add or subtract fractions with different denominators.
- Adding and Subtracting with the same denominator:

$$\frac{a}{b} + \frac{c}{b} = \frac{a+c}{b}$$
$$\frac{a}{b} - \frac{c}{b} = \frac{a-c}{b}$$

Adding and Subtracting fractions with different denominators:

$$\frac{a}{b} + \frac{c}{d} = \frac{ad+cb}{bd}$$
$$\frac{a}{b} - \frac{c}{d} = \frac{ad-cb}{bd}$$

Add fractions.

1) $\frac{2}{3} + \frac{1}{2}$

2) $\frac{3}{5} + \frac{1}{3}$

3) $\frac{5}{6} + \frac{1}{2}$

4) $\frac{7}{4} + \frac{5}{9}$

5) $\frac{2}{5} + \frac{1}{5}$

6) $\frac{3}{7} + \frac{1}{2}$

7) $\frac{3}{4} + \frac{2}{5}$

8) $\frac{2}{3} + \frac{1}{5}$

9) $\frac{16}{25} + \frac{3}{5}$

Subtract fractions.

10) $\frac{4}{5} - \frac{2}{5}$

11) $\frac{3}{5} - \frac{2}{7}$

12) $\frac{1}{2} - \frac{1}{3}$

13) $\frac{8}{9} - \frac{3}{5}$

14) $\frac{3}{7} - \frac{3}{14}$

15) $\frac{4}{15} - \frac{1}{10}$

16) $\frac{3}{4} - \frac{13}{18}$

17) $\frac{5}{8} - \frac{2}{5}$

18) $\frac{1}{2} - \frac{1}{9}$

2–3 Multiplying and Dividing Fractions

Helpful

Hints

- **Multiplying fractions:** multiply the top numbers and multiply the bottom numbers.
- **Divide fractions:** Keep, Change, Flip Keep first fraction, change division sign to multiplication, and flip the numerator and denominator of the second fraction. Then, solve!

Example:

$$\frac{a}{b} \times \frac{c}{d} = \frac{a \times c}{b \times d}$$

$$\frac{a}{b} \div \frac{c}{d} = \frac{a}{b} \times \frac{d}{c} = \frac{ad}{bc}$$

Multiplying fractions. Then simplify.

1) $\dfrac{1}{5} \times \dfrac{2}{3}$

2) $\dfrac{3}{4} \times \dfrac{2}{3}$

3) $\dfrac{2}{5} \times \dfrac{3}{7}$

4) $\dfrac{3}{8} \times \dfrac{1}{3}$

5) $\dfrac{3}{5} \times \dfrac{2}{5}$

6) $\dfrac{7}{9} \times \dfrac{1}{3}$

7) $\dfrac{2}{3} \times \dfrac{3}{8}$

8) $\dfrac{1}{4} \times \dfrac{1}{3}$

9) $\dfrac{5}{7} \times \dfrac{7}{12}$

Dividing fractions.

10) $\dfrac{2}{9} \div \dfrac{1}{4}$

11) $\dfrac{1}{2} \div \dfrac{1}{3}$

12) $\dfrac{6}{11} \div \dfrac{3}{4}$

13) $\dfrac{11}{14} \div \dfrac{1}{10}$

14) $\dfrac{3}{5} \div \dfrac{5}{9}$

15) $\dfrac{1}{2} \div \dfrac{1}{2}$

16) $\dfrac{3}{5} \div \dfrac{1}{5}$

17) $\dfrac{12}{21} \div \dfrac{3}{7}$

18) $\dfrac{5}{14} \div \dfrac{9}{10}$

2–4 Adding and Subtracting Mixed Numbers

Helpful

Hints

The steps are the same whether you're adding or subtracting mixed numbers:

- Find the Least Common Denominator (LCD)
- Find the equivalent fractions.
- Add the fractions and add the whole numbers.
- Write your answer in lowest terms.

Example:

$$1\frac{3}{4} + 2\frac{3}{8} = 4\frac{1}{8}$$

$$5\frac{2}{3} - 3\frac{2}{7} = 2\frac{8}{21}$$

Add.

1) $4\frac{1}{2} + 5\frac{1}{2}$

2) $2\frac{3}{8} + 3\frac{1}{8}$

3) $5\frac{3}{5} + 5\frac{1}{5}$

4) $1\frac{1}{3} + 2\frac{2}{3}$

5) $5\frac{1}{6} + 5\frac{1}{2}$

6) $3\frac{1}{3} + 1\frac{1}{3}$

7) $1\frac{10}{11} + 1\frac{1}{3}$

8) $2\frac{3}{6} + 1\frac{1}{2}$

9) $5\frac{3}{5} + 5\frac{1}{5}$

10) $7 + \frac{1}{5}$

11) $1\frac{5}{7} + \frac{1}{3}$

12) $2\frac{1}{4} + 1\frac{2}{4}$

Subtract.

13) $4\frac{1}{2} - 3\frac{1}{2}$

14) $3\frac{3}{8} - 3\frac{1}{8}$

15) $6\frac{3}{5} - 5\frac{1}{5}$

16) $2\frac{1}{3} - 1\frac{2}{3}$

17) $6\frac{1}{6} - 5\frac{1}{2}$

18) $3\frac{1}{3} - 1\frac{1}{3}$

19) $2\frac{10}{11} - 1\frac{1}{3}$

20) $2\frac{1}{2} - 1\frac{1}{2}$

21) $6\frac{3}{5} - 2\frac{1}{5}$

22) $7\frac{2}{5} - 1\frac{1}{5}$

23) $2\frac{5}{7} - 1\frac{1}{3}$

24) $2\frac{1}{4} - 1\frac{1}{2}$

2–5 Multiplying and Dividing Mixed Numbers

Helpful

Hints

1- Convert the mixed numbers to improper fractions.
2- Multiply or Divide fractions and simplify if necessary.

$$a\frac{c}{b} = a + \frac{c}{b} = \frac{ab+c}{b}$$

Example:

$$2\frac{1}{3} \times 5\frac{3}{7} =$$

$$\frac{7}{3} \times \frac{38}{7} = \frac{38}{3} = 12\frac{2}{3}$$

$$4\frac{1}{4} \div 2\frac{2}{3} = 1\frac{19}{32}$$

Find each product.

1) $1\frac{2}{3} \times 1\frac{1}{4}$

2) $1\frac{3}{5} \times 1\frac{2}{3}$

3) $1\frac{2}{3} \times 3\frac{2}{7}$

4) $4\frac{1}{8} \times 1\frac{2}{5}$

5) $2\frac{2}{5} \times 3\frac{1}{5}$

6) $1\frac{1}{3} \times 1\frac{2}{3}$

7) $1\frac{5}{8} \times 2\frac{1}{2}$

8) $3\frac{2}{5} \times 2\frac{1}{5}$

9) $2\frac{2}{3} \times 4\frac{1}{4}$

10) $2\frac{3}{5} \times 1\frac{2}{4}$

11) $1\frac{1}{3} \times 1\frac{1}{4}$

12) $3\frac{2}{5} \times 1\frac{1}{5}$

Find each quotient.

13) $2\frac{1}{5} \div 2\frac{1}{2}$

14) $2\frac{3}{5} \div 1\frac{1}{3}$

15) $3\frac{1}{6} \div 4\frac{2}{3}$

16) $1\frac{2}{3} \div 3\frac{1}{3}$

17) $4\frac{1}{8} \div 2\frac{2}{4}$

18) $3\frac{1}{2} \div 2\frac{3}{5}$

19) $3\frac{5}{9} \div 1\frac{2}{5}$

20) $2\frac{2}{7} \div 1\frac{1}{2}$

21) $3\frac{1}{5} \div 1\frac{1}{2}$

22) $4\frac{3}{5} \div 2\frac{1}{3}$

23) $6\frac{1}{6} \div 1\frac{2}{3}$

24) $2\frac{2}{3} \div 1\frac{1}{3}$

2–6 Adding and Subtracting Decimals

Helpful

Hints

1– Write down the numbers, one under the other, with the decimal points lined up.
2– Add zeros to have same number of digits for both numbers.
3– Add or Subtract using column addition or subtraction.

Example:

$$\begin{array}{r} 16.18 \\ - \ 13.45 \\ \hline 2.73 \end{array}$$

Add and subtract decimals.

1)
$$\begin{array}{r} 15.14 \\ - \ 12.18 \\ \hline \rule{2em}{0.4pt} \end{array}$$

3)
$$\begin{array}{r} 82.56 \\ + \ 12.28 \\ \hline \rule{2em}{0.4pt} \end{array}$$

5)
$$\begin{array}{r} 90.37 \\ + \ 56.97 \\ \hline \rule{2em}{0.4pt} \end{array}$$

2)
$$\begin{array}{r} 65.72 \\ + \ 43.67 \\ \hline \rule{2em}{0.4pt} \end{array}$$

4)
$$\begin{array}{r} 34.18 \\ - \ 23.45 \\ \hline \rule{2em}{0.4pt} \end{array}$$

6)
$$\begin{array}{r} 45.78 \\ - \ 23.39 \\ \hline \rule{2em}{0.4pt} \end{array}$$

Solve.

7) _____ + 1.3 = 4.8

8) 4.2 + _____ = 11.6

9) 9.9 + _____ = 16

10) 6.9 + _____ = 16.4

11) _____ + 5.1 = 8.6

12) _____ + 7.9 = 15.2

2–7 Multiplying and Dividing Decimals

Helpful

Hints

For Multiplication:
− Set up and multiply the numbers as you do with whole numbers.
− Count the total number of decimal places in both of the factors.
− Place the decimal point in the product.
For Division:
− If the divisor is not a whole number, move decimal point to right to make it a whole number. Do the same for dividend.
− Divide similar to whole numbers.
− Put decimal point directly above decimal point in the dividend.

Find each product.

1)
$$\begin{array}{r} 4.5 \\ \times\ 1.6 \\ \hline \end{array}$$

2)
$$\begin{array}{r} 7.7 \\ \times\ 9.9 \\ \hline \end{array}$$

3)
$$\begin{array}{r} 2.6 \\ \times\ 1.5 \\ \hline \end{array}$$

4)
$$\begin{array}{r} 8.9 \\ \times\ 9.7 \\ \hline \end{array}$$

5)
$$\begin{array}{r} 15.1 \\ \times\ 12.6 \\ \hline \end{array}$$

6)
$$\begin{array}{r} 6.9 \\ \times\ 3.3 \\ \hline \end{array}$$

7)
$$\begin{array}{r} 5.7 \\ \times\ 7.8 \\ \hline \end{array}$$

8)
$$\begin{array}{r} 98.20 \\ \times\ 100 \\ \hline \end{array}$$

9)
$$\begin{array}{r} 23.99 \\ \times\ 1000 \\ \hline \end{array}$$

Find each quotient.

10) $9.2 \div 3.6$

11) $27.6 \div 3.8$

12) $12.6 \div 4.7$

13) $6.5 \div 8.1$

14) $1.4 \div 10$

15) $3.6 \div 100$

16) $4.24 \div 10$

17) $14.6 \div 100$

2–8 Converting Between Fractions, Decimals and Mixed Numbers

Helpful

Hints

Fraction to Decimal:
– Divide the top number by the bottom number.
Decimal to Fraction:
– Write decimal over 1.
– Multiply both top and bottom by 10 for every number after the decimal point.
– Simplify.

Convert fractions to decimals.

1) $\dfrac{9}{10}$

2) $\dfrac{56}{100}$

3) $\dfrac{3}{4}$

4) $\dfrac{2}{5}$

5) $\dfrac{1}{3}$

6) $\dfrac{4}{5}$

7) $\dfrac{5}{6}$

8) $\dfrac{5}{8}$

9) $\dfrac{13}{21}$

Convert decimal into fraction.

10) 0.3

11) 4.5

12) 2.5

13) 2.3

14) 0.8

15) 0.25

16) 0.14

17) 0.2

18) 0.08

19) 0.45

20) 2.6

21) 5.2

2–9 Rounding Numbers

Helpful

Hints

Rounding is putting a number up or down to the nearest whole number or the nearest hundred, etc.

Example:
64 rounded to the nearest ten is 60, because 64 is closer to 60 than to 70.

Round each number to the underlined place value.

1) 9̲72

2) 2,9̲95

3) 36̲4

4) 8̲1

5) 5̲5

6) 33̲4

7) 1,2̲03

8) 9.5̲7

9) 7.4̲84

10) 9.1̲4

11) 3̲9

12) 9̲,123

13) 3,45̲2

14) 5̲69

15) 1,2̲30

16) 9̲8

17) 9̲3

18) 3̲7

19) 49̲3

20) 2,9̲23

21) 9̲,845

22) 5̲55

23) 9̲39

24) 6̲9

2–10 Factoring Numbers

Helpful

Hints

- Factoring numbers means to break the numbers into numbers that can be multiplied together to get the original number.
- First few prime numbers: 2, 3, 5, 7, 11, 13, 17, 19

Example:

$12 = 2 \times 2 \times 3$

List all positive factors of each number.

1) 68

2) 56

3) 24

4) 40

5) 86

6) 78

7) 50

8) 98

9) 45

10) 26

11) 54

12) 28

13) 55

14) 85

15) 50

List the prime factorization for each number.

16) 50

17) 25

18) 69

19) 21

20) 45

21) 68

22) 26

23) 86

24) 93

2–11 Prime Factorization

Helpful

Hints

- Prime Factorization is finding prime numbers that multiply together to get the original number.

Example:

18 = 2 x 3 x 3

Factor the following numbers to their prime factors.

1) 20

2) 12

3) 16

4) 27

5) 36

6) 42

7) 58

8) 35

9) 62

10) 49

11) 51

12) 78

13) 63

14) 77

15) 46

16) 69

17) 18

18) 32

19) 15

20) 33

21) 40

2–12 Greatest Common Factor

Helpful

Hints

- List the prime factors of each number.
- Multiply common prime factors.

Example:

$200 = 2 \times 2 \times 2 \times 5 \times 5$
$60 = 2 \times 2 \times 3 \times 5$
GCF $(200, 60) = 2 \times 2 \times 5 = 20$

Find the GCF for each number pair.

1) 20, 30

2) 4, 14

3) 5, 45

4) 68, 12

5) 5, 12

6) 15, 27

7) 3, 24

8) 34, 6

9) 4, 10

10) 5, 3

11) 6, 16

12) 30, 3

13) 24, 28

14) 70, 10

15) 45, 8

16) 90, 35

17) 78, 34

18) 55, 75

19) 60, 72

20) 100, 78

21) 30, 40

2–13 Least Common Multiple

Helpful

Hints

- Find the GCF for the two numbers.
- Divide that GCF into either number.
- Take that answer and multiply it by the other number.

Example:

LCM (200, 60):
GCF is 20
200 ÷ 20 = 10
10 × 60 = 600

Find the LCM for each number pair.

1) 4, 14

2) 5, 15

3) 16, 10

4) 4, 34

5) 8, 3

6) 12, 24

7) 9, 18

8) 5, 6

9) 8, 19

10) 9, 21

11) 19, 29

12) 7, 6

13) 25, 6

14) 4, 8

15) 30, 10, 50

16) 18, 36, 27

17) 12, 8, 18

18) 8, 18, 4

19) 26, 20, 30

20) 10, 4, 24

21) 15, 30, 45

2–14 Divisibility Rules

Helpful

Hints

- Divisibility means that a number can be divided by other numbers evenly.

Example:
24 is divisible by 6, because
24 ÷ 6 = 4

Use the divisibility rules to underline the answers.

8   <u>2</u> 3 <u>4</u> 5 6 7 <u>8</u> 9 10

1) 16   2 3 4 5 6 7 8 9 10

2) 10   2 3 4 5 6 7 8 9 10

3) 15   2 3 4 5 6 7 8 9 10

4) 28   2 3 4 5 6 7 8 9 10

5) 36   2 3 4 5 6 7 8 9 10

6) 15   2 3 4 5 6 7 8 9 10

7) 27   2 3 4 5 6 7 8 9 10

8) 70   2 3 4 5 6 7 8 9 10

9) 57   2 3 4 5 6 7 8 9 10

10) 102   2 3 4 5 6 7 8 9 10

11) 144   2 3 4 5 6 7 8 9 10

12) 75   2 3 4 5 6 7 8 9 10

Answers of Worksheets – Chapter 2

2–1 Simplifying Fractions

1) $\dfrac{11}{18}$

2) $\dfrac{4}{5}$

3) $\dfrac{2}{3}$

4) $\dfrac{3}{4}$

5) $\dfrac{1}{3}$

6) $\dfrac{1}{4}$

7) $\dfrac{4}{9}$

8) $\dfrac{1}{2}$

9) $\dfrac{2}{5}$

10) $\dfrac{1}{9}$

11) $\dfrac{5}{9}$

12) $\dfrac{3}{4}$

13) $\dfrac{5}{8}$

14) $\dfrac{13}{16}$

15) $\dfrac{1}{5}$

16) $\dfrac{4}{7}$

17) $\dfrac{1}{2}$

18) $\dfrac{5}{12}$

19) $\dfrac{3}{8}$

20) $\dfrac{1}{4}$

21) $\dfrac{5}{9}$

2–2 Adding and Subtracting Fractions

1) $\dfrac{7}{6}$

2) $\dfrac{14}{15}$

3) $\dfrac{4}{3}$

4) $\dfrac{83}{36}$

5) $\dfrac{3}{5}$

6) $\dfrac{13}{14}$

7) $\dfrac{23}{20}$

8) $\dfrac{13}{15}$

9) $\dfrac{31}{25}$

10) $\dfrac{2}{5}$

11) $\dfrac{11}{35}$

12) $\dfrac{1}{6}$

13) $\dfrac{13}{45}$

14) $\dfrac{3}{14}$

15) $\dfrac{1}{6}$

16) $\dfrac{1}{36}$

17) $\dfrac{9}{40}$

18) $\dfrac{7}{18}$

2–3 Multiplying and Dividing Fractions

1) $\dfrac{2}{15}$

2) $\dfrac{1}{2}$

3) $\dfrac{6}{35}$

4) $\dfrac{1}{8}$

5) $\dfrac{6}{25}$

6) $\dfrac{7}{27}$

7) $\dfrac{1}{4}$

8) $\dfrac{1}{12}$

9) $\dfrac{5}{12}$

10) $\dfrac{8}{9}$

11) $\dfrac{3}{2}$

12) $\dfrac{8}{11}$

13) $\dfrac{55}{7}$

14) $\dfrac{27}{25}$

15) 1

16) 3

17) $\dfrac{4}{3}$

18) $\dfrac{25}{63}$

2–4 Adding and Subtracting Mixed Numbers

1) 10

2) $5\dfrac{1}{2}$

3) $10\dfrac{4}{5}$

4) 4

5) $10\dfrac{2}{3}$

6) $4\dfrac{2}{3}$

7) $3\dfrac{8}{33}$

8) 4

9) $10\dfrac{4}{5}$

10) $7\dfrac{1}{5}$

11) $2\dfrac{1}{21}$

12) $3\dfrac{3}{4}$

13) 1

14) $\dfrac{1}{4}$

15) $1\dfrac{2}{5}$

16) $\dfrac{2}{3}$

17) $\dfrac{2}{3}$

18) 2

19) $1\dfrac{19}{33}$

20) 1

21) $4\dfrac{2}{5}$

22) $6\dfrac{1}{5}$

23) $1\dfrac{8}{21}$

24) $\dfrac{3}{4}$

2–5 Multiplying and Dividing Mixed Numbers

1) $2\frac{1}{12}$

2) $2\frac{2}{3}$

3) $5\frac{10}{21}$

4) $5\frac{31}{40}$

5) $7\frac{17}{25}$

6) $2\frac{2}{9}$

7) $4\frac{1}{16}$

8) $7\frac{12}{25}$

9) $11\frac{1}{3}$

10) $3\frac{9}{10}$

11) $1\frac{2}{3}$

12) $4\frac{2}{25}$

13) $\frac{22}{25}$

14) $1\frac{19}{20}$

15) $\frac{19}{28}$

16) $\frac{1}{2}$

17) $1\frac{13}{20}$

18) $1\frac{9}{26}$

19) $2\frac{34}{63}$

20) $1\frac{11}{20}$

21) $2\frac{2}{15}$

22) $1\frac{34}{35}$

23) $3\frac{7}{10}$

24) 2

2–6 Adding and Subtracting Decimals

1) 2.96

2) 109.39

3) 94.84

4) 10.73

5) 147.34

6) 22.39

7) 3.5

8) 7.4

9) 6.1

10) 9.5

11) 3.5

12) 7.3

2–7 Multiplying and Dividing Decimals

1) 7.2

2) 76.23

3) 3.9

4) 86.33

5) 190.26

6) 22.77

7) 44.46

8) 9820

9) 23990

10) 2.5555...

11) 7.2631...

12) 2.6808...

13) 0.8024...

14) 0.14

15) 0.036

16) 0.424

17) 0.146

2–8 Converting Between Fractions, Decimals and Mixed Numbers

1) 0.9

2) 0.56

3) 0.75

4) 0.4

5) 0.333…

6) 0.8

7) 0.8333…

8) 0.625

9) 0.6190…

10) $\frac{3}{10}$

11) $4\frac{1}{2}$

12) $2\frac{1}{2}$

13) $2\frac{3}{10}$

14) $\frac{4}{5}$

15) $\frac{1}{4}$

16) $\frac{7}{50}$

17) $\frac{1}{5}$

18) $\frac{2}{25}$

19) $\frac{9}{20}$

20) $2\frac{3}{5}$

21) $5\frac{1}{5}$

2–9 Rounding Numbers

1) 1,000

2) 3,000

3) 360

4) 80

5) 60

6) 330

7) 1,200

8) 9.6

9) 7.5

10) 9.1

11) 40

12) 9,000

13) 3,450

14) 600

15) 1,200

16) 100

17) 90

18) 40

19) 490

20) 2,900

21) 10,000

22) 560

23) 900

24) 70

2–10 Factoring Numbers

1) 1, 2, 4, 17, 34, 68
2) 1, 2, 4, 7, 8, 14, 28, 56
3) 1, 2, 3, 4, 6, 8, 12, 24
4) 1, 2, 4, 5, 8, 10, 20, 40
5) 1, 2, 43, 86

6) 1, 2, 3, 6, 13, 26, 39, 78
7) 1, 2, 5, 10, 25, 50
8) 1, 2, 7, 14, 49, 98
9) 1, 3, 5, 9, 15, 45
10) 1, 2, 13, 26

11) 1, 2, 3, 6, 9, 18, 27, 54

12) 1, 2, 4, 7, 14, 28

13) 1, 5, 11, 55

14) 1, 5, 17, 85

15) 1, 2, 5, 10, 25, 50

16) 2 × 5 × 5

17) 5 × 5

18) 3 × 23

19) 3 × 7

20) 3 × 3 × 5

21) 2 × 2 × 17

22) 2 × 13

23) 2 × 43

24) 3 × 31

2–11 Prime Factorization

1) 2 . 2 . 5

2) 2 . 2 . 3

3) 2 . 2 . 2 . 2

4) 3 . 3 . 3

5) 2 . 2 . 3 . 3

6) 2 . 3 . 7

7) 2 . 29

8) 5 . 7

9) 2 . 31

10) 7 . 7

11) 3 . 17

12) 2 . 3 . 13

13) 3 . 3 . 7

14) 7 . 11

15) 2 . 23

16) 3 . 23

17) 2 . 3 . 3

18) 2 . 2 . 2 . 2 . 2

19) 3 . 5

20) 3 . 11

21) 2 . 2 . 2 . 5

2–12 Greatest Common Factor

1) 10

2) 2

3) 5

4) 4

5) 1

6) 3

7) 3

8) 2

9) 2

10) 1

11) 2

12) 3

13) 4

14) 10

15) 1

16) 5

17) 2

18) 5

19) 12

20) 2

21) 10

2–13 Least Common Multiple

1) 28

2) 15

3) 80

4) 68

5) 24

6) 24

7) 18

8) 30

9) 152

10) 63   14) 8   18) 72

11) 551   15) 150   19) 780

12) 42   16) 108   20) 120

13) 150   17) 72   21) 90

2–14 Divisibility Rules

8   <u>2</u> 3 <u>4</u> 5 6 7 <u>8</u> 9 10

1) 16   <u>2</u> 3 <u>4</u> 5 6 7 <u>8</u> 9 10

2) 10   <u>2</u> 3 4 <u>5</u> 6 7 8 9 <u>10</u>

3) 15   2 <u>3</u> 4 <u>5</u> 6 7 8 9 10

4) 28   <u>2</u> 3 <u>4</u> 5 6 <u>7</u> 8 9 10

5) 36   <u>2</u> <u>3</u> <u>4</u> 5 <u>6</u> 7 8 <u>9</u> 10

6) 18   <u>2</u> <u>3</u> 4 5 <u>6</u> 7 8 <u>9</u> 10

7) 27   2 <u>3</u> 4 5 6 7 8 <u>9</u> 10

8) 70   <u>2</u> 3 4 <u>5</u> 6 <u>7</u> 8 9 <u>10</u>

9) 57   2 <u>3</u> 4 5 6 7 8 9 10

10) 102   <u>2</u> <u>3</u> 4 5 <u>6</u> 7 8 9 10

11) 144   <u>2</u> <u>3</u> <u>4</u> 5 <u>6</u> 7 <u>8</u> <u>9</u> 10

12) 75   2 <u>3</u> 4 <u>5</u> 6 7 8 9 10

Chapter 3: Real Numbers and Integers

3–1 Adding and Subtracting Integers

3–2 Multiplying and Dividing Integers

3–3 Ordering Integers and Numbers

3–4 Arrange, Order, and Comparing Integers

3–5 Order of Operations

3–6 Mixed Integer Computations

3–7 Absolute Value

3–8 Integers and Absolute Value

3–9 Classifying Real Numbers Venn Diagram

3–1 Adding and Subtracting Integers

Helpful

Hints

- **Integers:** {… , −3, −2, −1, 0, 1, 2, 3, …}
Includes: zero, counting numbers, and the negative of the counting numbers.
  − Add a positive integer by moving to the right on the number line.
  − Add a negative integer by moving to the left on the number line.
  − Subtract an integer by adding its opposite.

Example:

$12 + 10 = 22$

$25 − 13 = 12$

$(−24) + 12 = −12$

$(−14) + (−12) = −26$

$14 − (−13) = 27$

Find the sum.

1) $(−12) + (−4)$

2) $5 + (−24)$

3) $(−14) + 23$

4) $(−8) + (39)$

5) $43 + (−12)$

6) $(−23) + (−4) + 3$

7) $4 + (−12) + (−10) + (−25)$

8) $19 + (−15) + 25 + 11$

9) $(−9) + (−12) + (32 − 14)$

10) $4 + (−30) + (45 − 34)$

Find the difference.

11) $(−14) − (−9) − (18)$

12) $(−9) − (−25)$

13) $(−12) − (8)$

14) $(28) − (−4)$

15) $(34) − (2)$

16) $(55) − (−5) + (−4)$

17) $(9) − (2) − (−5)$

18) $(2) − (4) − (−15)$

19) $(23) − (4) − (−34)$

20) $(−45) − (−87)$

3–2 Multiplying and Dividing Integers

Helpful

Hints

(negative) × (negative) = positive

(negative) ÷ (negative) = positive

(negative) × (positive) = negative

(negative) ÷ (positive) = negative

(positive) × (positive) = positive

Examples:

$3 \times 2 = 6$

$3 \times -3 = -9$

$-2 \times -2 = 4$

$10 \div 2 = 5$

$-4 \div 2 = -2$

$-12 \div -6 = 3$

Find each product.

1) $(-8) \times (-2)$

2) 3×6

3) $(-4) \times 5 \times (-6)$

4) $2 \times (-6) \times (-6)$

5) $11 \times (-12)$

6) $10 \times (-5)$

7) 8×8

8) $(-8) \times (-9)$

9) $6 \times (-5) \times 3$

10) $6 \times (-1) \times 2$

Find each quotient.

11) $18 \div 3$

12) $(-24) \div 4$

13) $(-63) \div (-9)$

14) $54 \div 9$

15) $20 \div (-2)$

16) $(-66) \div (-11)$

17) $64 \div 8$

18) $(-121) \div 11$

19) $72 \div 9$

20) $16 \div 4$

3–3 Ordering Integers and Numbers

Helpful

Hints

To compare numbers, you can use number line! As you move from left to right on the number line, you find a bigger number!

Example:

Order integers from least to greatest.

$(-11, -13, 7, -2, 12)$

$-13 < -11 < -2 < 7 < 12$

Order each set of integers from least to greatest.

1) $-15, -19, 20, -4, 1$ ___, ___, ___, ___, ___, ___

2) $6, -5, 4, -3, 2$ ___, ___, ___, ___, ___, ___

3) $15, -42, 19, 0, -22$ ___, ___, ___, ___, ___, ___

4) $26, -91, 0, -13, 67, -55$ ___, ___, ___, ___, ___, ___

5) $-17, -71, 90, -25, -54, -39$ ___, ___, ___, ___, ___, ___

6) $98, 5, 46, 19, 77, 24$ ___, ___, ___, ___, ___, ___

Order each set of integers from greatest to least.

7) $-2, 5, -3, 6, -4$ ___, ___, ___, ___, ___, ___

8) $-37, 7, -17, 27, 47$ ___, ___, ___, ___, ___, ___

9) $32, -27, 19, -17, 15$ ___, ___, ___, ___, ___, ___

10) $68, 81, 21, -18, 94, 72$ ___, ___, ___, ___, ___, ___

3–4 Arrange, Order, and Comparing Integers

Helpful

Hints

When using a number line, numbers increase as you move to the right.

Examples:

$5 < 7$,

$-5 < -2$

$-18 < -12$

Arrange these integers in descending order.

1) $21, 71, -18, -10, 82$ ___, ___, ___, ___, ___, ___

2) $15, 11, 20, 12, -9, -5$ ___, ___, ___, ___, ___, ___

3) $-5, 20, 15, 9, -11$ ___, ___, ___, ___, ___, ___

4) $19, 18, -9, -6, -11$ ___, ___, ___, ___, ___, ___

5) $56, -34, -12, -5, 32$ ___, ___, ___, ___, ___, ___

Compare. Use >, =, <

6) -8 ____ 12 11) -56 ____ -58

7) -10 ____ -16 12) 78 ____ 87

8) 43 ____ 34 13) -92 ____ -102

9) 15 ____ -16 14) -12 ____ -12

10) -354 ____ -345 15) -721 ____ -821

3–5 Order of Operations

Helpful

Hints

- Use "order of operations" rule when there are more than one math operation.

- PEMDAS
(parentheses / exponents / multiply / divide / add / subtract)

Example:

$(12 + 4) \div (-4) = -4$

Evaluate each expression.

1) $(2 \times 2) + 5$

2) $24 - (3 \times 3)$

3) $(6 \times 4) + 8$

4) $25 - (4 \times 2)$

5) $(6 \times 5) + 3$

6) $64 - (2 \times 4)$

7) $25 + (1 \times 8)$

8) $(6 \times 7) + 7$

9) $48 \div (4 + 4)$

10) $(7 + 11) \div (-2)$

11) $9 + (2 \times 5) + 10$

12) $(5 + 8) \times \dfrac{3}{5} + 2$

13) $2 \times 7 - (\dfrac{10}{9 - 4})$

14) $(12 + 2 - 5) \times 7 - 1$

15) $(\dfrac{7}{5 - 1}) \times (2 + 6) \times 2$

16) $20 \div (4 - (10 - 8))$

17) $\dfrac{50}{4(5 - 4) - 3}$

18) $2 + (8 \times 2)$

3–6 Mixed Integer Computations

Helpful

Hints

It worth remembering:

(negative) × (negative) = positive

(negative) ÷ (negative) = positive

(negative) × (positive) = negative

(negative) ÷ (positive) = negative

(positive) × (positive) = positive

Example:

$(-5) + 6 = 1$

$(-3) \times (-2) = 6$

$(9) \div (-3) = -3$

Compute.

1) $(-70) \div (-5)$

2) $(-14) \times 3$

3) $(-4) \times (-15)$

4) $(-65) \div 5$

5) $18 \times (-7)$

6) $(-12) \times (-2)$

7) $\dfrac{(-60)}{(-20)}$

8) $24 \div (-8)$

9) $22 \div (-11)$

10) $\dfrac{(-27)}{3}$

11) $4 \times (-4)$

12) $\dfrac{(-48)}{12}$

13) $(-14) \times (-2)$

14) $(-7) \times (7)$

15) $\dfrac{-30}{-6}$

16) $(-54) \div 6$

17) $(-60) \div (-5)$

18) $(-7) \times (-12)$

19) $(-14) \times 5$

20) $88 \div (-8)$

3–7 Absolute Value

Helpful

Hints

Refers to the distance of a number from 0, the distances are positive. Therefore, absolute value of a number cannot be negative. $|-22| = 22$

Example:

$|12| \times |-2| = 24$

$$|x| = \begin{cases} x & for\ x \geq 0 \\ -x & for\ x < 0 \end{cases}$$

$|x| < n \Rightarrow -n < x < n$

$|x| > n \Rightarrow x < -n\ or\ x > n$

Evaluate.

1) $|-4| + |-12| - 7$

2) $|-5| + |-13|$

3) $-18 + |-5 + 3| - 8$

4) $|27| \div |9|$

5) $|-9| \div |-1|$

6) $|200| \div |-100|$

7) $|55| \div |11|$

8) $|36| \div |-6|$

9) $|25| \times |-5|$

10) $|-3| \times |-8|$

11) $|12| \times |-5|$

12) $|11| \times |-6|$

13) $|-8| \times |4|$

14) $|-9| \times |-7|$

15) $|43 - 67 + 9| + |-11| - 1$

16) $|-45 + 78| + |23| - |45|$

17) $75 + |-11 - 30| - |2|$

18) $|-3 + 15| + |9 + 4| - 1$

3–8 Integers and Absolute Value

Helpful

Hints

To find an absolute value of a number, just find it's distance from 0!

Example:

$|-6| = 6$
$|6| = 6$
$|-12| = 12$
$|12| = 12$

Write absolute value of each number.

1) -4

2) -7

3) -8

4) 4

5) 5

6) -10

7) 1

8) 6

9) 8

10) -2

11) -1

12) 10

13) 3

14) 7

15) -5

16) -3

17) -9

18) 2

19) 4

20) -6

21) 9

Evaluate.

22) $|-43| - |12| + 10$

23) $76 + |-15 - 45| - |3|$

24) $30 + |-62| - 46$

25) $|32| - |-78| + 90$

26) $|-35 + 4| + 6 - 4$

27) $|-4| + |-11|$

28) $|-6 + 3 - 4| + |7 + 7|$

29) $|-9| + |-19| - 5$

3–9 Classifying Real Numbers Venn Diagram

Helpful

Hints

Example: 0.25 = rational number and real number

Natural numbers: (also known as counting numbers) are the numbers that we use to count. It starts with 1, followed by 2, then 3, and so on.
Whole numbers are the natural numbers plus zero.
Integers include all whole numbers plus "negatives" of the natural numbers.
Rational numbers are numbers which can be written as a fraction. That means if we can write a given number as a fraction where the numerator and denominator are both integers; then it is a rational number.
Irrational numbers are all numbers which when written in decimal form does not repeat and does not terminate.
Real numbers include both the rational and irrational numbers

Identify all of the subsets of real number system to which each number belongs.

Example:

0.1259 : Rational number

$\sqrt{2}$: Irrational number

3 : Natural number, whole number, Integer, rational number

1) 0

2) -5

3) -8.5

4) $\sqrt{4}$

5) -10

6) 18

7) 6

8) π

9) $1\frac{2}{7}$

10) -1

11) $\sqrt{5}$

Answers of Worksheets – Chapter 3

3–1 Adding and Subtracting Integers

1) -16

2) -19

3) 9

4) 31

5) 31

6) -24

7) -43

8) 40

9) -3

10) -15

11) -23

12) 16

13) -20

14) 32

15) 32

16) 56

17) 12

18) 13

19) 53

20) 42

3–2 Multiplying and Dividing Integers

1) 16

2) 18

3) 120

4) 72

5) -132

6) -50

7) 64

8) 72

9) -90

10) -12

11) 6

12) -6

13) 7

14) 6

15) -10

16) 6

17) 8

18) -11

19) 8

20) 4

3–3 Ordering Integers and Numbers

1) $-19, -15, -4, 1, 20$

2) $-5, -3, 2, 4, 6$

3) $-42, -22, 0, 15, 19$

4) $-91, -55, -13, 0, 26, 67$

5) $-71, -54, -39, -25, -17, 90$

6) $5, 19, 24, 46, 77, 98$

7) $6, 5, -2, -3, -4$

8) $47, 27, 7, -17, -37$

9) $32, 19, 15, -17, -27$

10) $94, 81, 72, 68, 21, -18$

3–4 Arrange and Order, Comparing Integers

1) $82, 71, 21, -10, -18$

2) $20, 15, 12, 11, -5, -9$

3) $20, 15, 9, -5, -11$

4) $19, 18, -6, -9, -11$

5) $56, 32, -5, -12, -34$

6) $<$

7) $>$

8) $>$

9) $>$

10) $<$

11) $>$

12) $<$

13) $>$

14) $=$

15) $>$

3–5 Order of Operations

1) 9

2) 15

3) 32

4) 17

5) 33

6) 56

7) 33

8) 49

9) 6

10) -9

11) 29

12) 9.8

13) 12

14) 62

15) 28

16) 10

17) 50

18) 18

3–6 Mixed Integer Computations

1) 14

2) -42

3) 60

4) -13

5) -126

6) 24

7) 3

8) -3

9) -2

10) -9

11) -16

12) -4

13) 28

14) -49

15) 5

16) -9

17) 12

18) 84

19) -70

20) -11

3–7 Absolute Value

1) 9	7) 5	13) 32
2) 18	8) 6	14) 63
3) − 24	9) 125	15) 25
4) 3	10) 24	16) 11
5) 9	11) 60	17) 114
6) 2	12) 66	18) 24

3–8 Integers and Absolute Value

1) 4	11) 1	21) 9
2) 7	12) 10	22) 41
3) 8	13) 3	23) 133
4) 4	14) 7	24) 46
5) 5	15) 5	25) 44
6) 10	16) 3	26) 33
7) 1	17) 9	27) 15
8) 6	18) 2	28) 21
9) 8	19) 4	29) 23
10) 2	20) 6	

3–9 Classifying Real Numbers Venn Diagram

1) 0: whole number, integer, rational number
2) − 5: integer, rational number
3) − 8.5: rational number
4) $\sqrt{4}$: natural number, whole number, integer, rational number
5) − 10: integer, rational number
6) 18 : natural number, whole number, integer, rational number
7) 6: natural number, whole number, integer, rational number
8) π: irrational number
9) $1\frac{2}{7}$: rational number
10)   − 1: integer, rational number
11) $\sqrt{5}$: irrational number

Chapter 4: Percent

4–1 Converting Between Percent, Fractions, and Decimals

Helpful

Hints

− To a percent: Move the decimal point 2 places to the right and add the % symbol.
− Divide by 100 to convert a number from percent to decimal.

Examples:

30% = 0.3

0.24 = 24%

Converting fractions to decimals.

1) $\dfrac{50}{100}$

2) $\dfrac{38}{100}$

3) $\dfrac{15}{100}$

4) $\dfrac{80}{100}$

5) $\dfrac{7}{100}$

6) $\dfrac{35}{100}$

7) $\dfrac{90}{100}$

8) $\dfrac{20}{100}$

9) $\dfrac{7}{100}$

Write each decimal as a percent.

10) 0.5

11) 0.9

12) 0.002

13) 0.524

14) 0.1

15) 0.03

16) 3.63

17) 0.008

18) 4.78

4–2 Percentage Calculations

Helpful

Hints

- Use the following formula to find part, whole, or percent

$$\text{part} = \frac{\text{percent}}{100} \times \text{whole}$$

Example:

$$\frac{20}{100} \times 100 = 20$$

Calculate the percentages.

1) 50% of 25

2) 80% of 15

3) 30% of 34

4) 70% of 45

5) 10% of 0

6) 80% of 22

7) 65% of 8

8) 78% of 54

9) 50% of 80

10) 20% of 10

11) 40% of 40

12) 90% of 0

13) 20% of 70

14) 55% of 60

15) 80% of 10

16) 20% of 880

17) 70% of 100

18) 80% of 90

Solve.

19) 50 is what percentage of 75?

20) What percentage of 100 is 70

21) Find what percentage of 60 is 35.

22) 40 is what percentage of 80?

4–3 Find What Percentage a Number Is of Another

Helpful

Hints

PERCENT: the number with the percent sign (%).
PART: the number with the word "is".
WHOLE: the number with the word "of".
– Divide the Part by the Base.
– Convert the answer to percent.

Example:

20 is what percent of 50?

$20 \div 50 = 0.40 = 40\%$

Find the percentage of the numbers.

1) 45 is what percent of 90?

2) 15 is what percent of 75?

3) 20 is what percent of 400?

4) 18 is what percent of 90?

5) 3 is what percent of 15?

6) 8 is what percent of 80?

7) 11 is what percent of 55?

8) 9 is what percent of 90?

9) 2.5 is what percent of 10?

10) 5 is what percent of 25?

11) 60 is what percent of 20?

12) 12 is what percent of 48?

13) 14 is what percent of 28?

14) 8.2 is what percent of 32.8?

15) 1200 is what percent of 4,800?

16) 4,000 is what percent of 20,000?

17) 45 is what percent of 900?

18) 10 is what percent of 200?

19) 15 is what percent of 60?

20) 1.2 is what percent of 24?

4–4 Find a Percentage of a Given Number

Helpful

Hints

- Use following formula to find part, whole, or percent

$$part = \frac{percent}{100} \times whole$$

Example:

$$\frac{50}{100} \times 50 = 25$$

Find a Percentage of a Given Number.

1) 90% of 50

2) 40% of 50

3) 10% of 0

4) 80% of 80

5) 60% of 40

6) 50% of 60

7) 30% of 20

8) 35% of 10

9) 10% of 80

10) 10% of 60

11) 100% 0f 50

12) 90% of 34

13) 80% of 42

14) 90% of 12

15) 20% of 56

16) 40% of 40

17) 40% of 6

18) 70% of 38

19) 30% of 3

20) 40% of 50

21) 100% of 8

4–5 Percent Problems

Helpful

Hints

Base = Part ÷ Percent
Part = Percent × Base
Percent = Part ÷ Base

Example:
2 is 10% of 20.
2 ÷ 0.10 = 20
2 = 0.10 × 20
0.10 = 2 ÷ 20

Solve each problem.

1) 51 is 340% of what?

2) 93% of what number is 97?

3) 27% of 142 is what number?

4) What percent of 125 is 29.3?

5) 60 is what percent of 126?

6) 67 is 67% of what?

7) 67 is 13% of what?

8) 41% of 78 is what?

9) 1 is what percent of 52.6?

10) What is 59% of 14 m?

11) What is 90% of 130 inches?

12) 16 inches is 35% of what?

13) 90% of 54.4 hours is what?

14) What percent of 33.5 is 21?

15) Liam scored 22 out of 30 marks in Algebra, 35 out of 40 marks in science and 89 out of 100 marks in mathematics. In which subject his percentage of marks in best?

16) Ella require 50% to pass her test. If she gets 280 marks and falls short by 20 marks, what were the maximum marks she could have got?

4–6 Percent of Increase and Decrease

Helpful

Hints

– To calculate the percentage increase:
New Number – Original Number
The result ÷ Original Number × 100
If your answer is a negative number, then this is a percentage decrease.

To calculate percentage decrease:
Original Number – New Number
The result ÷ Original Number × 100

Example:
From 84 miles to 24 miles

= 71.43% decrease

Find each percent change to the nearest percent, increase or decrease.

1) From 32 grams to 82 grams.

2) From 150 m to 45 m

3) From $438 to $443

4) From 256 ft to 140 ft

5) From 6469 ft to 7488 ft

6) From 36 inches to 90 inches

7) From 54 ft to 104 ft

8) From 84 miles to 24 miles

9) The population of a place in a particular year increased by 15%. Next year it decreased by 15%. Find the net increase or decrease percent in the initial population.

10) The salary of a doctor is increased by 40%. By what percent should the new salary be reduced in order to restore the original salary?

Answers of Worksheets – Chapter 4

4–1 Converting Between Percent, Fractions, and Decimals

1) 0.5	6) 0.35	11) 90%	16) 363%
2) 0.38	7) 0.9	12) 0.2%	17) 0.8%
3) 0.15	8) 0.2	13) 52.4%	18) 478%
4) 0.8	9) 0.07	14) 10%	
5) 0.07	10) 50%	15) 3%	

4–2 Percentage Calculations

1) 12.5	7) 5.2	13) 14	19) 67%
2) 12	8) 42.12	14) 33	20) 70%
3) 10.2	9) 40	15) 8	21) 58%
4) 31.5	10) 2	16) 176	22) 50%
5) 0	11) 16	17) 70	
6) 17.6	12) 0	18) 72	

4–3 Find What Percentage a Number Is of Another

1) 45 is what percent of 90? 50 %	8) 9 is what percent of 90? 10 %
2) 15 is what percent of 75? 20 %	9) 2.5 is what percent of 10? 25 %
3) 20 is what percent of 400? 5 %	10) 5 is what percent of 25? 20 %
4) 18 is what percent of 90? 20 %	11) 60 is what percent of 20? 300 %
5) 3 is what percent of 15? 20 %	12) 12 is what percent of 48? 25 %
6) 8 is what percent of 80? 10 %	13) 14 is what percent of 28? 50 %
7) 11 is what percent of 55? 20 %	14) 8.2 is what percent of 32.8? 25 %

15) 1200 is what percent of 4,800? 25%

16) 4,000 is what percent of 20,000? 20 %

17) 45 is what percent of 900? 5 %

18) 10 is what percent of 200? 5 %

19) 15 is what percent of 60? 25 %

20) 1.2 is what percent of 24? 5 %

4–4 Find a Percentage of a Given Number

1) 45

2) 20

3) 0

4) 64

5) 24

6) 30

7) 6

8) 3.5

9) 8

10) 6

11) 50

12) 30.6

13) 33.6

14) 10.8

15) 11.2

16) 16

17) 2.4

18) 26.6

19) 0.9

20) 20

21) 8

4–5 Percent Problems

1) 15

2) 104.3

3) 38.34

4) 23.44%

5) 47.6%

6) 100

7) 515.4

8) 31.98

9) 1.9%

10) 8.3 m

11) 117 inches

12) 45.7 inches

13) 49 hours

14) 62.7%

15) Mathematics

16) 600

4–6 Percent of Increase and Decrease

1) 156.25% increase

2) 70% decrease

3) 1.142% increase

4) 45.31% decrease

5) 15.75% increase

6) 150% increase

7) 92.6% increase

8) 71.43% decrease

9) 2.25% decrease

10) $28\frac{4}{7}$ %

60

Chapter 5: Algebraic Expressions

5–1 Expressions and Variables

5–2 Simplifying Variable Expressions

5–3 The Distributive Property

5–4 Translate Phrases into an Algebraic Statement

5–5 Evaluating One Variable

5–6 Evaluating Two Variables

5–7 Combining like Terms

5–1 Expressions and Variables

Helpful

Hints

A variable is a letter that represents unknown numbers. A variable can be used in the same manner as all other numbers:

Addition	$2 + a$	2 plus a
Subtraction	$y - 3$	y minus 3
Division	$\dfrac{4}{x}$	4 divided by x
Multiplication	$5a$	5 times a

Simplify each expression.

1) $x + 5x$,

   use $x = 5$

2) $8(-3x + 9) + 6$,

   use $x = 6$

3) $10x - 2x + 6 - 5$,

   use $x = 5$

4) $2x - 3x - 9$,

   use $x = 7$

5) $(-6)(-2x - 4y)$,

   use $x = 1$, $y = 3$

6) $8x + 2 + 4y$,

   use x = 9, $y = 2$

7) $(-6)(-8x - 9y)$,

   use $x = 5$, $y = 5$

8) $6x + 5y$,

   use $x = 7$, $y = 4$

Simplify each expression.

9) $5(-4 + 2x)$

10) $-3 - 5x - 6x + 9$

11) $6x - 3x - 8 + 10$

12) $(-8)(6x - 4) + 12$

13) $9(7x + 4) + 6x$

14) $(-9)(-5x + 2)$

5–2 Simplifying Variable Expressions

Helpful

Hints

Remove parentheses by multiplying factors.
Use exponent rules to remove parentheses in terms with exponents.
Combine like terms by adding coefficients.
Combine the constants.

Example:

$2x + 2(1 - 5x) =$

$2x + 2 - 10x = -8x + 2$

Simplify each expression.

1) $-2 - x^2 - 6x^2$

2) $3 + 10x^2 + 2$

3) $8x^2 + 6x + 7x^2$

4) $5x^2 - 12x^2 + 8x$

5) $2x^2 - 2x - x$

6) $(-6)(8x - 4)$

7) $4x + 6(2 - 5x)$

8) $10x + 8(10x - 6)$

9) $9(-2x - 6) - 5$

10) $3(x + 9)$

11) $7x + 3 - 3x$

12) $2.5x^2 \times (-8x)$

Simplify.

13) $-2(4 - 6x) - 3x$, $x = 1$

14) $2x + 8x$, $x = 2$

15) $9 - 2x + 5x + 2$, $x = 5$

16) $5(3x + 7)$, $x = 3$

17) $2(3 - 2x) - 4$, $x = 6$

18) $5x + 3x - 8$, $x = 3$

19) $x - 7x$, $x = 8$

20) $5(-2 - 9x)$, $x = 4$

5–3 The Distributive Property

Helpful

Hints

Distributive Property:
$a\,(b\,+\,c)\,=\,ab\,+\,ac$

Example:

$3\,(4\,+\,3x)$

$=\,12\,+\,9x$

Use the distributive property to simply each expression.

1) $-\,(-\,2\,-\,5x)$

2) $(-\,6x\,+\,2)(-1)$

3) $(-\,5)\,(x\,-\,2)$

4) $-\,(7\,-\,3x)$

5) $8\,(8\,+\,2x)$

6) $2\,(12\,+\,2x)$

7) $(-\,6x\,+\,8)\,4$

8) $(3\,-\,6x)(-\,7)$

9) $(-\,12)\,(2x\,+\,1)$

10) $(8\,-\,2x)\,9$

11) $(-\,2x)\,(-\,1\,+\,9x)\,-\,4x\,(4\,+\,5x)$

12) $3\,(-\,5x\,-\,3)\,+\,4(6\,-\,3x)$

13) $(-\,2)(x\,+\,4)\,-\,(2\,+\,3x)$

14) $(-\,4)(3x\,-\,2)\,+\,6\,(x\,+\,1)$

15) $(-\,5)(4x\,-\,1)\,+\,4\,(x\,+\,2)$

16) $(-\,3)(x\,+\,4)\,-\,(2\,+\,3x)$

5–4 Translate Phrases into an Algebraic Statement

Helpful

Hints

Translating key words and phrases into algebraic expressions:
Addition: plus, more than, the sum of, etc.
Subtraction: minus, less than, decreased, etc.
Multiplication: times, product, multiplied, etc.
Division: quotient, divided, ratio, etc.
Example:
eight more than a number is 20
$8 + x = 20$

Write an algebraic expression for each phrase.

1) A number increased by forty–two.

2) The sum of fifteen and a number

3) The difference between fifty–six and a number.

4) The quotient of thirty and a number.

5) Twice a number decreased by 25.

6) Four times the sum of a number and − 12.

7) A number divided by − 20.

8) The quotient of 60 and the product of a number and − 5.

9) Ten subtracted from a number.

10) The difference of six and a number.

5–5 Evaluating One Variable

Helpful

Hints

– To evaluate one variable expression, find the variable and substitute a number for that variable.

– Perform the arithmetic operations.

Example:

$4x + 8, x = 6$

$4(6) + 8 = 24 + 8$

$= 32$

Simplify each algebraic expression.

1) $9 - x$, $x = 3$

2) $x + 2$, $x = 5$

3) $3x + 7$, $x = 6$

4) $x + (-5)$, $x = -2$

5) $3x + 6$, $x = 4$

6) $4x + 6$, $x = -1$

7) $10 + 2x - 6$, $x = 3$

8) $10 - 3x$, $x = 8$

9) $\dfrac{20}{x} - 3$, $x = 5$

10) $(-3) + \dfrac{x}{4} + 2x$, $x = 16$

11) $(-2) + \dfrac{x}{7}$, $x = 21$

12) $(-\dfrac{14}{x}) - 9 + 4x$, $x = 2$

13) $(-\dfrac{6}{x}) - 9 + 2x$, $x = 3$

14) $(-2) + \dfrac{x}{8}$, $x = 16$

15) $8(5x - 12)$, $x = -2$

5–6 Evaluating Two Variables

Helpful

Hints

To evaluate an algebraic expression, substitute a number for each variable and perform the arithmetic operations.

Example:

$2x + 4y - 3 + 2,$
$x = 5, y = 3$
$2(5) + 4(3) - 3 + 2$
$= 10$
$+ 12 - 3$
$+ 2 = 21$

Simplify each algebraic expression.

1) $2x + 4y - 3 + 2,$

   $x = 5, y = 3$

2) $(-\dfrac{12}{x}) + 1 + 5y,$

   $x = 6, y = 8$

3) $(-4)(-2a - 2b),$

   $a = 5, b = 3$

4) $10 + 3x + 7 - 2y,$

   $x = 7, y = 6$

5) $9x + 2 - 4y,$

   $x = 7, y = 5$

6) $6 + 3(-2x - 3y),$

   $x = 9, y = 7$

7) $12x + y,$

   $x = 4, y = 8$

8) $x \times 4 \div y,$

   $x = 3, y = 2$

9) $2x + 14 + 4y,$

   $x = 6, y = 8$

10) $4a - (5 - b),$

    $a = 4, b = 6$

5–7 Combining like Terms

Helpful

Hints

- Terms are separated by + and − signs.
- Like terms are terms with same variables and same powers.
- Be sure to use the + or − that is in front of the coefficient.

Example:

$22x + 6 + 2x =$

$24x + 6$

Simplify each expression.

1) $5 + 2x - 8$

2) $(-2x + 6)\,2$

3) $7 + 3x + 6x - 4$

4) $(-4) - (3)(5x + 8)$

5) $9x - 7x - 5$

6) $x - 12x$

7) $7\,(3x + 6) + 2x$

8) $(-11x) - 10x$

9) $3x - 12 - 5x$

10) $13 + 4x - 5$

11) $(-22x) + 8x$

12) $2\,(4 + 3x) - 7x$

13) $(-4x) - (6 - 14x)$

14) $5\,(6x - 1) + 12x$

15) $22x + 6 + 2x$

16) $(-13x) - 14x$

17) $(-6x) - 9 + 15x$

18) $(-6x) + 7x$

19) $(-5x) + 12 + 7x$

20) $(-3x) - 9 + 15x$

21) $20x - 19x$

Answers of Worksheets – Chapter 5

5–1 Expressions and Variables

1) 30
2) −66
3) 41
4) −16
5) 84

6) 82
7) 510
8) 62
9) $10x - 20$
10) $6 - 11x$

11) $3x + 2$
12) $44 - 48x$
13) $69x + 36$
14) $45x - 18$

5–2 Simplifying Variable Expressions

1) $-7x^2 - 2$
2) $10x^2 + 5$
3) $15x^2 + 6x$
4) $-7x^2 + 8x$
5) $2x^2 - 3x$
6) $-48x + 24$
7) $-26x + 12$

8) $90x - 48$
9) $-18x - 59$
10) $3x + 27$
11) $4x + 3$
12) $-20x^3$
13) 1
14) 20

15) 26
16) 80
17) -22
18) 16
19) -48
20) -190

5–3 The Distributive Property

1) $5x + 2$
2) $6x - 2$
3) $-5x + 10$
4) $3x - 7$
5) $16x + 64$
6) $4x + 24$

7) $-24x + 32$
8) $42x - 21$
9) $-24x - 12$
10) $-18x + 72$
11) $-38x^2 - 14x$
12) $-27x + 15$

13) $-5x - 10$
14) $-6x + 14$
15) $-16x + 13$
16) $-6x - 14$

5–4 Translate Phrases into an Algebraic Statement

1) $x + 42$

2) $15 + x$

3) $56 - x$

4) $30/x$

5) $2x - 25$

6) $4(x + (-12))$

7) $\dfrac{x}{-20}$

8) $\dfrac{60}{-5x}$

9) $x - 10$

10) $6 - x$

5–5 Evaluating One Variable

1) 6

2) 7

3) 25

4) –7

5) 18

6) 2

7) 10

8) –14

9) 1

10) 33

11) 1

12) –8

13) –5

14) 0

15) –176

5–6 Evaluating Two Variables

1) 21

2) 39

3) 64

4) 26

5) 45

6) –111

7) 56

8) 6

9) 58

10) 17

5–7 Combining like Terms

1) $2x - 3$

2) $-4x + 12$

3) $9x + 3$

4) $-15x - 28$

5) $2x - 5$

6) $-11x$

7) $23x + 42$

8) $-21x$

9) $-2x - 12$

10) $4x + 8$

11) $-14x$

12) $-x + 8$

13) $10x - 6$

14) $42x - 5$

15) $24x + 6$

16) $-27x$

17) $9x - 9$

18) x

19) $2x + 12$

20) $12x - 9$

21) x

Chapter 6: Equations

6–1 One–Step Equations

Helpful

Hints

- The values of two mathematical expressions are equal in an equation.

$$ax + b = c$$

- You will only need to perform one operation in order to solve the equation.

Example:

$-8x = 16$

$x = -2$

Solve each equation.

1) x + 3 = 17

2) 22 = (− 8) + x

3) 3x = (− 30)

4) (− 36) = (− 6x)

5) (− 6) = 4 + x

6) 2 + x = (− 2)

7) 20x − (− 220)

8) 18 = x + 5

9) (− 23) + x = (− 19)

10) 5x = (− 45)

11) x − 12 = (− 25)

12) x − 3 = (− 12)

13) (− 35) = x − 27

14) 8 − 2x

15) (− 6x) = 36

16) (− 55) = (− 5x)

17) x − 30 = 20

18) 8x = 32

19) 36 = (− 4x)

20) 4x = 68

21) 30x = 300

6–2 One–Step Equation Word Problems

Helpful

Hints

– Define the variable.
– Translate key words and phrases into math equation.
– Isolate the variable and solve the equation.

Solve.

1) How many boxes of envelopes can you buy with $18 if one box costs $3?

2) After paying $6.25 for a salad, Ella has $45.56. How much money did she have before buying the salad?

3) How many packages of diapers can you buy with $50 if one package costs $5?

4) Last week James ran 20 miles more than Michael. James ran 56 miles. How many miles did Michael run?

5) Last Friday Jacob had $32.52. Over the weekend he received some money for cleaning the attic. He now has $44. How much money did he receive?

6) After paying $10.12 for a sandwich, Amelia has $35.50. How much money did she have before buying the sandwich?

6–3 Two–Step Equations

Helpful

Hints

– You will only need to perform two operations (add, subtract, multiply, or divide) in order to solve the equation.
– Simplify using the inverse of addition or subtraction.
– Simplify further by using the inverse of multiplication or division.

Example:

$-2(x-1) = 42$

$(x-1) = -21$

$x = -20$

Solve each equation.

1) $5(8+x) = 20$

2) $(-7)(x-9) = 42$

3) $(-12)(2x-3) = (-12)$

4) $6(1+x) = 12$

5) $12(2x+4) = 60$

6) $7(3x+2) = 42$

7) $8(14+2x) = (-34)$

8) $(-15)(2x-4) = 48$

9) $3(x+5) = 12$

10) $\dfrac{3x-12}{6} = 4$

11) $(-12) = \dfrac{x+15}{6}$

12) $110 = (-5)(2x-6)$

13) $\dfrac{x}{8} - 12 = 4$

14) $20 = 12 + \dfrac{x}{4}$

15) $\dfrac{-24+x}{6} = (-12)$

16) $(-4)(5+2x) = (-100)$

17) $(-12x) + 20 = 32$

18) $\dfrac{-2+6x}{4} = (-8)$

19) $\dfrac{x+6}{5} = (-5)$

20) $(-9) + \dfrac{x}{4} = (-15)$

6–4 Two–Step Equation Word Problems

Helpful

Hints

– Translate the word problem into equations with variables.
– Solve the equations to find the solutions to the word problems.

Solve.

1) The sum of three consecutive even numbers is 48. What is the smallest of these numbers?

2) How old am I if 400 reduced by 2 times my age is 244?

3) For a field trip, 4 students rode in cars and the rest filled nine buses. How many students were in each bus if 472 students were on the trip?

4) The sum of three consecutive numbers is 72. What is the smallest of these numbers?

5) 331 students went on a field trip. Six buses were filled, and 7 students traveled in cars. How many students were in each bus?

6) You bought a magazine for $5 and four erasers. You spent a total of $25. How much did each eraser cost?

6–5 Multi–Step Equations

Helpful

Hints

– Combine "like" terms on one side.
– Bring variables to one side by adding or subtracting.
– Simplify using the inverse of addition or subtraction.
– Simplify further by using the inverse of multiplication or division.

Example:

$$3x + 15 = -2x + 5$$
Add 2x both sides
$$5x + 15 = +5$$
Subtract 15 both sides
$$5x = -10$$
Divide by 5 both sides
$$x = -2$$

Solve each equation.

1) $-(2 - 2x) = 10$

2) $-12 = -(2x + 8)$

3) $3x + 15 = (-2x) + 5$

4) $-28 = (-2x) - 12x$

5) $2(1 + 2x) + 2x = -118$

6) $3x - 18 = 22 + x - 3 + x$

7) $12 - 2x = (-32) - x + x$

8) $7 - 3x - 3x = 3 - 3x$

9) $6 + 10x + 3x = (-30) + 4x$

10) $(-3x) - 8(-1 + 5x) = 352$

11) $24 = (-4x) - 8 + 8$

12) $9 = 2x - 7 + 6x$

13) $6(1 + 6x) = 294$

14) $-10 = (-4x) - 6x$

15) $4x - 2 = (-7) + 5x$

16) $5x - 14 = 8x + 4$

17) $40 = -(4x - 8)$

18) $(-18) - 6x = 6(1 + 3x)$

19) $x - 5 = -2(6 + 3x)$

20) $6 = 1 - 2x + 5$

Answers of Worksheets – Chapter 6

6–1 One–Step Equations

1) 14	8) 13	15) -6
2) 30	9) 4	16) 11
3) -10	10) -9	17) 50
4) 6	11) -13	18) 4
5) -10	12) -9	19) -9
6) -4	13) -8	20) 17
7) -11	14) 4	21) 10

6–2 One–Step Equation Word Problems

1) 6	3) 10	5) 11.48
2) $51.81	4) 36	6) 45.62

6–3 Two–Step Equations

1) -4	8) $\frac{2}{5}$	15) -48
2) 3	9) -1	16) 10
3) 2	10) 12	17) -1
4) 1	11) -87	18) -5
5) 0.5	12) -8	19) -31
6) $\frac{4}{3}$	13) 128	20) -24
7) $-\frac{73}{8}$	14) 32	

6–4 Two–Step Equation Word Problems

1) 14	3) 52	5) 54
2) 78	4) 23	6) $5

6–5 Multi–Step Equations

1) 6
2) 2
3) -2
4) 2
5) -20
6) 37
7) 22

8) $\frac{4}{3}$
9) -4
10) -8
11) -6
12) 2
13) 8

14) 1
15) 5
16) -6
17) -8
18) -1
19) -1
20) 0

Chapter 7: Proportions and Ratios

7–1 Writing Ratios

7–2 Simplifying Ratios

7–3 Proportional Ratios

7–4 Create a Proportion

7–5 Similar Figures

7–6 Similar Figure Word Problems

7–7 Ratio and Rates Word Problems

7–1 Writing Ratios

Helpful

Hints

- A ratio is a comparison of two numbers. Ratio can be written as a division.

Example:

$3 : 5$, or $\frac{3}{5}$

Express each ratio as a rate and unite rate.

1) 120 miles on 4 gallons of gas.

2) 24 dollars for 6 books.

3) 200 miles on 14 gallons of gas

4) 24 inches of snow in 8 hours

Express each ratio as a fraction in the simplest form.

5) 3 feet out of 30 feet

6) 18 cakes out of 42 cakes

7) 16 dimes t0 24 dimes

8) 12 dimes out of 48 coins

9) 14 cups to 84 cups

10) 45 gallons to 65 gallons

11) 10 miles out of 40 miles

12) 22 blue cars out of 55 cars

13) 32 pennies to 300 pennies

14) 24 beetles out of 86 insects

7–2 Simplifying Ratios

Helpful

Hints

– You can calculate equivalent ratios by multiplying or dividing both sides of the ratio by the same number.

Examples:

$3 : 6 = 1 : 2$

$4 : 9 = 8 : 18$

Reduce each ratio.

1) 21 : 49

2) 20 : 40

3) 10: 50

4) 14: 18

5) 45: 27

6) 49: 21

7) 100: 10

8) 12 : 8

9) 35 : 45

10) 8: 20

11) 25: 35

12) 21 : 27

13) 52 : 82

14) 12: 36

15) 24 : 3

16) 15: 30

17) 3 : 36

18) 8 : 16

19) 6 : 100

20) 2 : 20

21) 10: 60

22) 14: 63

23) 68: 80

24) 8: 80

7–3 Proportional Ratios

Helpful

Hints

- A proportion means that two ratios are equal. It can be written in two ways:

$$\frac{a}{b} = \frac{c}{d} , \ a : b = c : d$$

Example:

$$\frac{9}{3} = \frac{6}{d}$$

$$d = 2$$

Solve each proportion.

1) $\frac{3}{6} = \frac{8}{d}$

2) $\frac{k}{5} = \frac{12}{15}$

3) $\frac{30}{5} = \frac{12}{x}$

4) $\frac{x}{2} = \frac{1}{8}$

5) $\frac{d}{3} = \frac{2}{6}$

6) $\frac{27}{7} = \frac{30}{x}$

7) $\frac{8}{5} = \frac{k}{15}$

8) $\frac{60}{20} = \frac{3}{d}$

9) $\frac{x}{3} = \frac{12}{18}$

10) $\frac{25}{5} = \frac{x}{8}$

11) $\frac{12}{x} = \frac{4}{2}$

12) $\frac{x}{4} = \frac{18}{2}$

13) $\frac{80}{10} = \frac{k}{10}$

14) $\frac{12}{6} = \frac{6}{d}$

15) $\frac{x}{4} = \frac{30}{5}$

16) $\frac{9}{5} = \frac{k}{5}$

17) $\frac{45}{15} = \frac{15}{d}$

18) $\frac{60}{x} = \frac{10}{3}$

19) $\frac{d}{3} = \frac{14}{6}$

20) $\frac{k}{4} = \frac{4}{2}$

21) $\frac{4}{2} = \frac{x}{7}$

7–4 Create a Proportion

Helpful

A proportion contains 2 equal fractions! A proportion is simply a statement that two fractions are equal.

Example:

2, 4, 8, 16

Hints

$$\frac{2}{4} = \frac{8}{16}$$

Create proportion from the given set of numbers.

1) 1, 6, 2, 3

2) 12, 144, 1, 12

3) 16, 4, 8, 2

4) 9, 5, 27, 15

5) 7, 10, 60, 42

6) 8, 7, 24, 21

7) 10, 5, 8, 4

8) 3, 12, 8, 2

9) 2, 2, 1, 4

10) 3, 6, 7, 14

11) 2, 6, 5, 15

12) 7, 2, 14, 4

7–5 Similar Figures

Helpful

Hints

Two or more figures are similar if they have the same shape. The corresponding angles are equal, and the corresponding sides are in proportion.

Example:

3–4–5 triangle is

similar to a

6–8–10 triangle

Each pair of figures is similar. Find the value of x.

1)

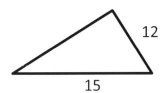 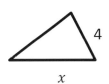

2)

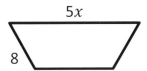 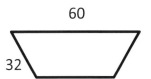

3)

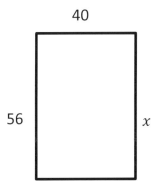 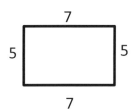

7–6 Similar Figure Word Problems

Helpful

Hints

To solve a similarity word problem, create a proportion and use cross multiplication method!

Example:

$$\frac{x}{4} = \frac{8}{16}$$

$$16x = 4 \times 8$$

Answer each question and round your answer to the nearest whole number.

1) If a 42.9 ft tall flagpole casts a 253.1 ft long shadow, then how long is the shadow that a 6.2 ft tall woman casts?

2) A model igloo has a scale of 1 in : 2 ft. If the real igloo is 10 ft wide, then how wide is the model igloo?

3) If a 18 ft tall tree casts a 9 ft long shadow, then how tall is an adult giraffe that casts a 7 ft shadow?

4) Find the distance between San Joe and Mount Pleasant if they are 2 cm apart on a map with a scale of 1 cm : 9 km.

5) A telephone booth that is 8 ft tall casts a shadow that is 4 ft long. Find the height of a lawn ornament that casts a 2 ft shadow.

7–7 Ratio and Rates Word Problems

Solve.

1) In a party, 10 soft drinks are required for every 12 guests. If there are 252 guests, how many soft drink is required?

2) In Jack's class, 18 of the students are tall and 10 are short. In Michael's class 54 students are tall and 30 students are short. Which class has a higher ratio of tall to short students?

3) Are these ratios equivalent?
   12 cards to 72 animals, 11 marbles to 66 marbles

4) The price of 3 apples at the Quick Market is $1.44. The price of 5 of the same apples at Walmart is $2.50. Which place is the better buy?

5) The bakers at a Bakery can make 160 bagels in 4 hours. How many bagels can they bake in 16 hours? What is that rate per hour?

6) You can buy 5 cans of green beans at a supermarket for $3.40. How much does it cost to buy 35 cans of green beans?

Answers of Worksheets – Chapter 7

7–1 Writing Ratios

1) $\frac{120\ miles}{4\ gallons}$, 30 miles per gallon

2) $\frac{36\ dollars}{6\ books}$, 6.00 dollars per book

3) $\frac{200\ miles}{14\ gallons}$, 14.29 miles per gallon

4) $\frac{24"\ of\ snow}{8\ hours}$, 4.83 inches of snow per hour

5) $\frac{1}{10}$

6) $\frac{3}{7}$

7) $\frac{2}{3}$

8) $\frac{1}{4}$

9) $\frac{1}{6}$

10) $\frac{9}{13}$

11) $\frac{1}{4}$

12) $\frac{2}{5}$

13) $\frac{8}{75}$

14) $\frac{12}{43}$

7–2 Simplifying Ratios

1) 3 : 7

2) 1 : 2

3) 1 : 5

4) 7 : 9

5) 5 : 3

6) 7 : 3

7) 10 : 1

8) 3 : 2

9) 7 : 9

10) 2 : 5

11) 5 : 7

12) 7 : 9

13) 26 : 41

14) 1 : 3

15) 8 : 1

16) 1 : 2

17) 1 : 12

18) 1 : 2

19) 3 : 50

20) 1 : 10

21) 1 : 6

22) 2 : 9

23) 17 : 20

24) 1 : 10

7–3 Proportional Ratios

1) 16	8) 1	15) 24
2) 4	9) 2	16) 9
3) 2	10) 40	17) 5
4) 0.25	11) 6	18) 18
5) 1	12) 36	19) 7
6) 7.78	13) 80	20) 8
7) 24	14) 3	21) 14

7–4 Create a Proportion

1) $1 : 3 = 2 : 6$	6) $7 : 21 = 8 : 24$	11) $5 : 2 = 15 : 6$
2) $12 : 144 = 1 : 12$	7) $8 : 10 = 4 : 5$	12) $7 : 2 = 14 : 4$
3) $2 : 4 = 8 : 16$	8) $2 : 3 = 8 : 12$	13) $6 : 7 = 24 : 28$
4) $5 : 15 = 9 : 27$	9) $4 : 2 = 2 : 1$	
5) $7 : 42, 10 : 60$	10) $7 : 3 = 14 : 6$	

7–5 Similar Figures

1) 5	2) 3	3) 56

7–6 Similar Figure Word Problems

1) 36.6 ft	3) 14 ft	5) 4 ft
2) 5 in	4) 18 km	

7–7 Ratio and Rates Word Problems

1) 210

2) The ratio for both class is equal to 9 to 5.

3) Yes! Both ratios are 1 to 6.

4) The price at the Quick Market is a better buy.

5) 640, the rate is 40 per hour.

6) $23.80

Chapter 8: Inequalities

8–1 Graphing Single – Variable Inequalities

Helpful

Hints

– Isolate the variable.
– Find the value of the inequality on the number line.
– For less than or greater than draw open circle on the value of the variable.
– If there is an equal sign too, then use filled circle.
– Draw a line to the right direction.

Draw a graph for each inequality.

1) $-2 > x$

2) $5 \leq -x$

3) $x > 7$

4) $-x > 1.5$

8–2 One–Step Inequalities

Helpful

Hints

– Isolate the variable.
– For dividing both sides by negative numbers, flip the direction of the inequality sign.

Example:
x + 4 ≥ 11
x ≥ 7

Solve each inequality and graph it.

1) $x + 9 \geq 11$

2) $x - 4 \leq 2$

3) $6x \geq 36$

4) $7 + x < 16$

5) $x + 8 \leq 1$

6) $3x > 12$

7) $3x < 24$

8–3 Two–Step Inequalities

Helpful

Hints

– Isolate the variable.
– For dividing both sides by negative numbers, flip the direction of the of the inequality sign.
– Simplify using the inverse of addition or subtraction.
– Simplify further by using the inverse of multiplication or division.

Example:
$2x + 9 \geq 11$
$2x \geq 2$
$x \geq 1$

Solve each inequality and graph it.

1) $3x - 4 \leq 5$

2) $4x - 19 < 19$

3) $3x + 6 \geq 12$

4) $6x - 5 \geq 19$

5) $2x - 3 < 21$

6) $3 + 4x < 19$

8–4 Multi–Step Inequalities

Helpful

Hints

– Isolate the variable.
– Simplify using the inverse of addition or subtraction.
– Simplify further by using the inverse of multiplication or division.

Example:

$$\frac{7x + 1}{3} \geq 5$$

$$7x + 1 \geq 15$$

$$7x \geq 14$$

$$x \geq 7$$

Solve each inequality and graph it.

1) $\dfrac{7x + 1}{3} \geq 5$

2) $\dfrac{9x}{7} - x < 2$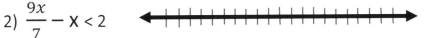

3) $\dfrac{4x + 8}{2} \leq 12$

4) $\dfrac{3x - 8}{7} > 1$

5) $-3 (x - 7) > 21$

6) $4 + \dfrac{x}{3} < 7$

Answers of Worksheets – Chapter 8

8–1 Graphing Single–Variable Inequalities

1) $-2 > x$
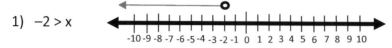

2) $x \leq -5$

3) $x > 7$
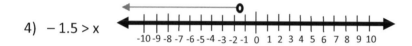

4) $-1.5 > x$

8–2 One–Step Inequalities

1) $x + 9 \geq 11$

2) $x - 4 \leq 2$

3) $6x \geq 36$
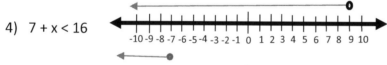

4) $7 + x < 16$

5) $x + 8 \leq 1$
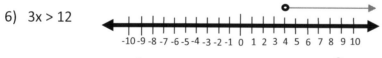

6) $3x > 12$
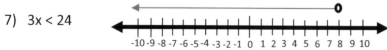

7) $3x < 24$

8–3 Two–Step Inequalities

1) $3x - 4 \leq 5$

2) $4x + 19 < 19$

3) $3x + 6 \geq 12$

4) $6x - 5 \geq 19$

5) $2x - 3 < 11$

6) $3 + 4x < 19$

8–4 Multi–Step Inequalities

1) $\dfrac{7x+1}{3} \geq 5$

2) $\dfrac{9x}{7} - x < 2$

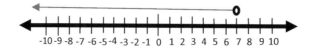

3) $\dfrac{4x+8}{2} \leq 12$

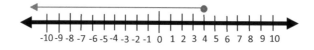

4) $\dfrac{3x-8}{7} > 1$

5) $-3(x-7) > 21$

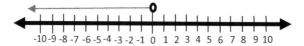

6) $4 + \dfrac{x}{3} < 7$

Chapter 9: Exponents and Radicals

9–1 Multiplication Property of Exponents

9–2 Division Property of Exponents

9–3 Powers of Products and Quotients

9–4 Zero and Negative Exponents

9–5 Negative Exponents and Negative Bases

9–6 Writing Scientific Notation

9–7 Square Roots

9–1 Multiplication Property of Exponents

Helpful

Hints

Exponents rules

$x^a \cdot x^b = x^{a+b}$ $x^a/x^b = x^{a-b}$

$1/x^b = x^{-b}$ $(x^a)^b = x^{a \cdot b}$

$(xy)^a = x^a \cdot y^a$

Example:

$(x^2 y)^3 = x^6 y^3$

Simplify.

1) $4^2 \cdot 4^2$

2) $2 \cdot 2^2 \cdot 2^2$

3) $3^2 \cdot 3^2$

4) $3x^3 \cdot x$

5) $12x^4 \cdot 3x$

6) $6x \cdot 2x^2$

7) $5x^4 \cdot 5x^4$

8) $6x^2 \cdot 6x^3 y^4$

9) $7x^2 y^5 \cdot 9xy^3$

10) $7xy^4 \cdot 4x^3 y^3$

11) $(2x^2)^2$

12) $3x^5 y^3 \cdot 8x^2 y^3$

13) $7x^3 \cdot 10y^3 x^5 \cdot 8yx^3$

14) $(x^4)^3$

15) $(2x^2)^4$

16) $(x^2)^3$

17) $(6x)^2$

18) $3x^4 y^5 \cdot 7x^2 y^3$

9–2 Division Property of Exponents

Helpful $\frac{x^a}{x^b} = x^{a-b}$, $x \neq 0$

Example:

$\frac{x^{12}}{x^5} = x^7$

Hints

Simplify.

1) $\frac{5^5}{5}$

2) $\frac{3}{3^5}$

3) $\frac{2^2}{2^3}$

4) $\frac{2^4}{2^2}$

5) $\frac{x}{x^3}$

6) $\frac{3x^3}{9x^4}$

7) $\frac{2x^{-5}}{9x^{-2}}$

8) $\frac{21x^8}{7x^3}$

9) $\frac{4x^6}{7x^7}$

10) $\frac{4x^2}{6x^3}$

11) $\frac{5x}{10x^3}$

12) $\frac{2x^3}{3x^5}$

13) $\frac{12x^3}{14x^6}$

14) $\frac{9x^3}{12y^8}$

15) $\frac{25xy^4}{5x^6y^2}$

16) $\frac{2x^4}{7x}$

17) $\frac{16x^2y^8}{4x^3}$

18) $\frac{12x^4}{15x^7y^9}$

19) $\frac{12yx^4}{10yx^8}$

20) $\frac{16x^4y}{9x^8y^2}$

21) $\frac{5x^8}{20x^8}$

9–3 Powers of Products and Quotients

Helpful

Hints

For any nonzero numbers
a and b and any integer x,
$(ab)^x = a^x \cdot b^x$.

Example:

$(2x^2 \cdot y^3)^2 = 4x^2 \cdot y^6$

Simplify.

1) $(2x^3)^4$

2) $(4xy^4)^2$

3) $(5x^4)^2$

4) $(11x^5)^2$

5) $(4x^2y^4)^4$

6) $(2x^4y^4)^3$

7) $(3x^2y^2)^2$

8) $(3x^4y^3)^4$

9) $(2x^6y^8)^2$

10) $(12x\ 3x)^3$

11) $(2x^9\ x^6)^3$

12) $(5x^{10}y^3)^3$

13) $(4x^3\ x^2)^2$

14) $(3x^3\ 5x)^2$

15) $(10x^{11}y^3)^2$

16) $(9x^7\ y^{\ 5})^2$

17) $(4x^4y^6)^5$

18) $(4x^4)^2$

19) $(3x\ 4y^3)^2$

20) $(9x^2y)^3$

21) $(12x^2y^5)^2$

9–4 Zero and Negative Exponents

Helpful

Hints

A negative exponent simply means that the base is on the wrong side of the fraction line, so you need to flip the base to the other side to make the power positive. For instance, "x^{-3}" just means "x^3" but in the denominator side, as in $\dfrac{1}{x^2}$

Example:

$5^{-2} = \dfrac{1}{25}$

Evaluate the following expressions.

1) 8^{-2}

2) 2^{-4}

3) 10^{-2}

4) 5^{-3}

5) 22^{-1}

6) 9^{-1}

7) 3^{-2}

8) 4^{-2}

9) 5^{-2}

10) 35^{-1}

11) 6^{-3}

12) 0^{15}

13) 10^{-9}

14) 3^{-4}

15) 5^{-2}

16) 2^{-3}

17) 3^{-3}

18) 8^{-1}

19) 7^{-3}

20) 6^{-2}

21) $\left(\dfrac{2}{3}\right)^{-2}$

22) $\left(\dfrac{1}{5}\right)^{-3}$

23) $\left(\dfrac{1}{2}\right)^{-8}$

24) $\left(\dfrac{2}{5}\right)^{-3}$

9–5 Negative Exponents and Negative Bases

Helpful

Hints

– Make the power positive. A negative exponent is the reciprocal of that number with a positive exponent.

– The parenthesis is important!

– 5^{-1} is not the same as $(-5)^{-1}$

– $5^{-1} = -\frac{1}{5}$ and $(-5)^{-1} = +\frac{1}{5}$

Example:

$2x^{-3} = \dfrac{2}{x^3}$

Simplify.

1) -6^{-1}

2) $-4x^{-3}$

3) $-\dfrac{5x}{x^{-3}}$

4) $-\dfrac{a^{-3}}{b^{-2}}$

5) $-\dfrac{5}{x^{-3}}$

6) $\dfrac{7b}{-9c^{-4}}$

7) $-\dfrac{5n^{-2}}{10p^{-3}}$

8) $\dfrac{4ab^{-2}}{-3c^{-2}}$

9) $-12x^2y^{-3}$

10) $\left(-\dfrac{1}{3}\right)^{-2}$

11) $\left(-\dfrac{3}{4}\right)^{-2}$

12) $\left(\dfrac{3a}{2c}\right)^{-2}$

13) $\left(-\dfrac{5x}{3yz}\right)^{-3}$

14) $-\dfrac{2x}{a^{-4}}$

9–6 Writing Scientific Notation

Helpful

Hints

– It is a way of stating very big or very small numbers in decimal form.
– In scientific notation all numbers are written in the form of:
$$m \times 10^n$$

Decimal notation	Scientific notation
5	5×10^0
−25,000	-2.5×10^4
0.5	5×10^{-1}
2,122.456	$2,122456 \times 10^3$

Write each number in scientific notation.

1) 91×10^3

2) 60

3) 2000000

4) 0.0000006

5) 354000

6) 0.000325

7) 2.5

8) 0.00023

9) 56000000

10) 2000000

11) 78000000

12) 0.0000022

13) 0.00012

14) 0.004

15) 78

16) 1600

17) 1450

18) 130000

19) 60

20) 0.113

21) 0.02

9–7 Square Roots

Helpful

Hints

− A square root of x is a number r whose square is: $r^2 = x$

      r is a square root of x.

Example:

$\sqrt{4} = 2$

Find the value each square root.

1) $\sqrt{1}$

2) $\sqrt{4}$

3) $\sqrt{9}$

4) $\sqrt{25}$

5) $\sqrt{16}$

6) $\sqrt{49}$

7) $\sqrt{36}$

8) $\sqrt{0}$

9) $\sqrt{64}$

10) $\sqrt{81}$

11) $\sqrt{121}$

12) $\sqrt{225}$

13) $\sqrt{144}$

14) $\sqrt{100}$

15) $\sqrt{256}$

16) $\sqrt{289}$

17) $\sqrt{324}$

18) $\sqrt{400}$

19) $\sqrt{900}$

20) $\sqrt{529}$

21) $\sqrt{90}$

Answers of Worksheets – Chapter 9

9–1 Multiplication Property of Exponents

1) 4^4

2) 2^5

3) 3^4

4) $3x^4$

5) $36x^5$

6) $12x^3$

7) $25x^8$

8) $36x^5y^4$

9) $63x^3y^8$

10) $28x^4y^7$

11) $4x^4$

12) $24x^7y^6$

13) $560x^{11}y^4$

14) x^{12}

15) $16x^8$

16) x^6

17) $36x^2$

18) $21x^6y^8$

9–2 Division Property of Exponents

1) 5^4

2) $\dfrac{1}{3^4}$

3) $\dfrac{1}{2}$

4) 2^2

5) $\dfrac{1}{x^2}$

6) $\dfrac{1}{3x}$

7) $\dfrac{2}{9x^3}$

8) $3x^5$

9) $\dfrac{4}{7x}$

10) $\dfrac{2}{3x}$

11) $\dfrac{1}{2x^2}$

12) $\dfrac{2}{3x^2}$

13) $\dfrac{6}{7x^3}$

14) $\dfrac{3x^3}{4y^8}$

15) $\dfrac{5y^2}{x^5}$

16) $\dfrac{2x^3}{7}$

17) $\dfrac{4y^8}{x}$

18) $\dfrac{4}{5x^3y^9}$

19) $\dfrac{6}{5x^4}$

20) $\dfrac{16}{9x^4y}$

21) $\dfrac{1}{4}$

9–3 Powers of Products and Quotients

1) $16x^{12}$

2) $16x^2y^8$

3) $25x^8$

4) $121x^{10}$

5) $256x^8y^{16}$

6) $8x^{12}y^{12}$

7) $9x^4y^4$

8) $81x^{16}y^{12}$

9) $4x^{12}y^{16}$

10) $46.656x^6$

11) $8x^{45}$

12) $125x^{30}y^9$

13) $16x^{10}$

14) $225x^8$

15) $100x^{22}y^6$

16) $81x^{14}y^{10}$

17) $1,024x^{20}y^{30}$

18) $16x^8$

19) $144x^2y^6$

20) $729x^6y^3$

21) $144x^4y^{10}$

9–4 Zero and Negative Exponents

1) $\frac{1}{64}$

2) $\frac{1}{16}$

3) $\frac{1}{100}$

4) $\frac{1}{125}$

5) $\frac{1}{22}$

6) $\frac{1}{9}$

7) $\frac{1}{9}$

8) $\frac{1}{16}$

9) $\frac{1}{25}$

10) $\frac{1}{35}$

11) $\frac{1}{216}$

12) 0

13) $\frac{1}{1000000000}$

14) $\frac{1}{81}$

15) $\frac{1}{25}$

16) $\frac{1}{8}$

17) $\frac{1}{27}$

18) $\frac{1}{8}$

19) $\frac{1}{343}$

20) $\frac{1}{36}$

21) $\frac{9}{4}$

22) 125

23) 256

24) $\frac{125}{8}$

9–5 Negative Exponents and Negative Bases

1) $-\frac{1}{6}$

2) $-\frac{4}{x^3}$

3) $-5x^4$

4) $-\frac{b^2}{a^3}$

5) $-5x^3$

6) $-\frac{7bc^4}{9}$

7) $-\frac{p^3}{2n^2}$

8) $-\frac{4ac^2}{3b^2}$

9) $-\frac{12x^2}{y^3}$

10) 9

11) $\frac{16}{9}$

12) $\frac{4c^2}{9a^2}$

13) $-\frac{27y^3z^3}{125x^3}$

14) $-2xa^4$

9–6 Writing Scientific Notation

1) 9.1×10^4

2) 6×10^1

3) 2×10^6

4) 6×10^{-7}

5) 3.54×10^5

6) 3.25×10^{-4}

7) 2.5×10^0

8) 2.3×10^{-4}

9) 5.6×10^7

10) 2×10^6

11) 7.8×10^7

12) 2.2×10^{-6}

13) 1.2×10^{-4}

14) 4×10^{-3}

15) 7.8×10^1

16) 1.6×10^3

17) 1.45×10^3

18) 1.3×10^5

19) 6×10^1

20) 1.13×10^{-1}

21) 2×10^{-2}

9–7 Square Roots

1) 1

2) 2

3) 3

4) 5

5) 4

6) 7

7) 6

8) 0

9) 8

10) 9

11) 11

12) 15

13) 12

14) 10

15) 16

16) 17

17) 18

18) 20

19) 30

20) 23

21) $3\sqrt{10}$

Chapter 10: Measurements

10 –1 Inches and Centimeters

Helpful

Hints

1inch = 2.5 cm
1 foot = 12 inch
1 yard = 3 foot
1 yard = 36 inch
1 inch = 0.0254 m

Example:

18 inches = 0.4572 m

Convert to the units.

1inch = 2.5 cm

1) 25 cm = _____ inches

2) 11 inches = _____ cm

3) 1 m = _____ inches

4) 80 inches = _____ m

5) 200 cm = _____ m

6) 5 m = _____ cm

7) 4 feet = _____ inches

8) 10 yards = _____ inches

9) 16 feet = _____ inches

10) 48 inches = _____ Feet

11) 4 inches = _____ cm

12) 12.5 cm = _____ inches

13) 6 feet: _____ inches

14) 10 feet: _____ inches

15) 12 yards: _____ feet

16) 7 yards: _____ feet

10 –2 Metric Units

Helpful

Hints

1 m = 100 cm
1 cm = 10 mm
1 m = 1000 mm
1 km = 1000 m

Example:

12 cm = 0.12 m

Convert to the units.

1) 4 mm = _____ cm

2) 0.6 m = _____ mm

3) 2 m = _____ cm

4) 0.03 km = _____ m

5) 3000 mm = _____ km

6) 5 cm = _____ m

7) 0.03 m = _____ cm

8) 1000 mm = _____ km

9) 600 mm = _____ m

10) 0.77 km = _____ mm

11) 0.08 km = _____ m

12) 0.30 m = _____ cm

13) 400 m = _____ km

14) 5000 cm = _____ km

15) 40 mm = _____ cm

16) 800 m = _____ km

10 –3 Distance Measurement

Helpful

Hints

1 mile = 5280 ft
1 mile = 1760 yd
1 mile = 1609.34 m

Example:

10 miles = 52800 ft

Convert to the new units.

1) 2 mi = _____ ft

2) 21 mi = _____ ft

3) 6 mi = _____ ft

4) 3 mi = _____ yd

5) 72 mi = _____ ft

6) 41 mi = _____ yd

7) 62 mi = _____ yd

8) 39 mi = _____ yd

9) 7 mi = _____ yd

10) 94 mi = _____ yd

11) 87 mi = _____ yd

12) 23 mi = _____ yd

13) 2 mi = _____ m

14) 5 mi = _____ m

15) 6 mi = _____ m

16) 3 mi = _____ m

10 –4 Weight Measurement

Helpful

Hints

1 kg = 1000g

Example:

2000 g = 2 kg

Convert to grams.

1) 0.5 kg = _____ g

2) 3.2 kg = _____ g

3) 8.2 kg = _____ g

4) 9.2 kg = _____ g

5) 35 kg = _____ g

6) 87 kg = _____ g

7) 45 kg = _____ g

8) 15 kg = _____ g

9) 0.32 kg = _____ g

10) 81 kg = _____ g

Convert to kilograms.

11) 200,000 g = _____ kg

12) 30,000 g = _____ kg

13) 800,000 g = _____ kg

14) 20,000 g = _____ kg

15) 40,000 g = _____ kg

16) 500,000 g = _____ kg

Answers of Worksheets – Chapter 10

10–1 Inches & Centimeters

1) 25 cm = 9.84 inches

2) 11 inch = 27.94 cm

3) 1 m = 39.37 inches

4) 80 inch = 2.03 m

5) 200 cm = 2 m

6) 5 m = 500 cm

7) 4 feet = 48 inches

8) 10 yards = 360 inches

9) 16 feet = 192 inches

10) 48 inches = 4 Feet

11) 4 inch = 10.16 cm

12) 12.5 cm = 4.92 inches

13) 6 feet: 72 inches

14) 10 feet: 120 inches

15) 12 yards: 36 feet

16) 7 yards: 21 feet

10–2 Metric Units

1) 4 mm = 0.4 cm

2) 0.6 m = 600 mm

3) 2 m = 200 cm

4) 0.03 km = 30 m

5) 3000 mm = 0.003 km

6) 5 cm = 0.05 m

7) 0.03 m = 3 cm

8) 1000 mm = 0.001 km

9) 600 mm = 0.6 m

10) 0.77 km = 770,000 mm

11) 0.08 km = 80 m

12) 0.30 m = 30 cm

13) 400 m = 0.4 km

14) 5000 cm = 0.05 km

15) 40 mm = 4 cm

16) 800 m = 0.8 km

10–3 Distance Measurement

1) 21 mi = 110880 ft

2) 6 mi = 31680 ft

3) 3 mi = 5280 yd

4) 72 mi = 380160 ft

5) 41 mi = 72160 yd

6) 62 mi = 109120 yd

7) 39 mi = 68640 yd

8) 7 mi = 12320 yd

9) 94 mi = 165440 yd

10) 87 mi = 153120 yd

11) 23 mi = 40480 yd

12) 2 mi = 3218.69 m

13) 5 mi = 8046.72 m

14) 6 mi = 9656.06 m

15) 3 mi = 4828.03 m

10–4 Weight Measurement

1) 0.5 kg = 500 g

2) 3.2 kg = 3200 g

3) 8.2 kg = 8200 g

4) 9.2 kg = 9200 g

5) 35 kg = 35000 g

6) 87 kg = 87000 g

7) 45 kg = 45000 g

8) 15 kg = 15000 g

9) 0.32 kg = 320 g

10) 81 kg = 81000 g

11) 200,000 g = 200 kg

12) 30,000 g = 30 kg

13) 800,000 g = 800 kg

14) 20,000 g = 20 kg

15) 40,000 g = 40 kg

16) 500,000 g = 500 kg

Chapter 11: Plane Figures

11–1 Transformations: Translations, Rotations, and Reflections

11–2 The Pythagorean Theorem

11–3 Area of Triangles

11–4 Perimeter of Polygons

11–5 Area and Circumference of Circles

11–6 Area of Squares, Rectangles, and Parallelograms

11–7 Area of Trapezoids

11 −1 Transformations: Translations, Rotations, and Reflections

Helpful
Hints

- **Transformation:** A movement of a figure with certain properties.
- **Translation:** Moving every point in a shape in a specified direction.
- **Reflection:** The mirror image of a shape across an axis or a plane of reflection.
- **Rotation:** A transformation in a plane or a space that is the motion of a body around a fixed point.

Graph the image of the figure using the transformation given.

1) translation: 4 units right
   and 1 unit down

2) translation: 4 units right
   and 2 unit up

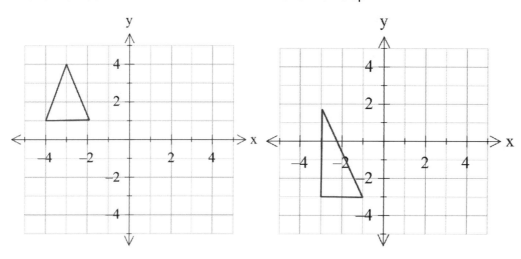

3) rotation 90∘ counterclockwise
   about the origin

4) rotation 180∘ about the origin

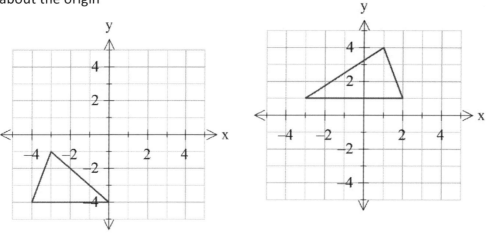

11–2 The Pythagorean Theorem

Helpful

Hints

– In any right triangle:

$$a^2 + b^2 = c^2$$

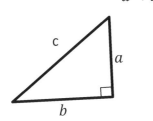

Example:

Missing side = 5

$$3^2 + 4^2 = x^2$$
$$9 + 16 = x^2$$
$$25 = x^2$$
$$x = 5$$

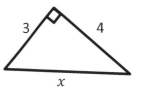

Do the following lengths form a right triangle?

1)

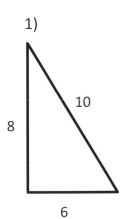

2)   3)

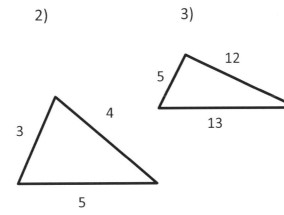

Find each missing length to the nearest tenth.

4)

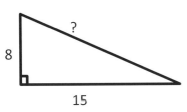

5)

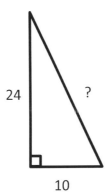

6)

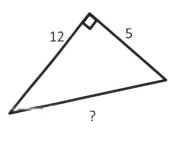

11 –3 Area of Triangles

Helpful

Hints

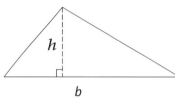

$$\text{Area} = \frac{1}{2} \, b \, . \, h$$

Find the area of each.

1)

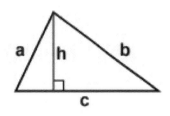

c = 9 mi

h = 3.7 mi

2)

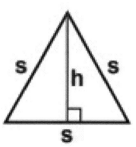

s = 14 m

h = 8 m

3)

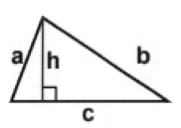

a = 5 m

b = 11 m

c = 14 m

h = 4 m

4)

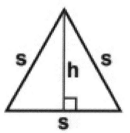

s = 16 m

h = 12.1 m

11 –4 Perimeter of Polygons

Helpful

Hints

Perimeter of a square = 4s

s

Perimeter of a rectangle
$= 2(length \ + \ width)$

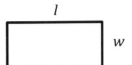

l

w

Find the perimeter of each shape.

1)

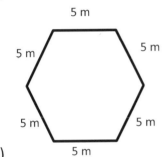

5 m

5 m

5 m

5 m

5 m

5 m

2)

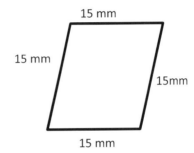

15 mm

15 mm

15mm

15 mm

3)

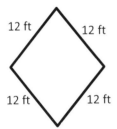

12 ft

12 ft

12 ft

12 ft

4)

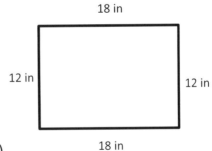

18 in

12 in

12 in

18 in

5)

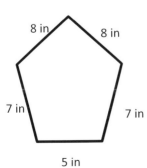

8 in

8 in

7 in

7 in

5 in

6)

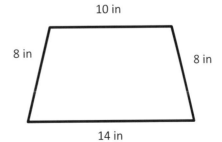

10 in

8 in

8 in

14 in

11 –5 Area and Circumference of Circles

Helpful

Hints

Area = πr²
Circumference = 2πr

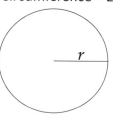

Example:

If the radius of a circle is 3, then:
Area = πr² = (3.14) (3)² = 28.26
Circumference = 2πr = 2(3.14) (3) = 18.84

Find the area and circumference of each.

1)

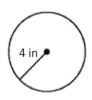

4 in

2)

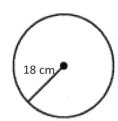

18 cm

3)

5 m

4)

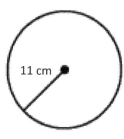

11 cm

5)

8 km

6)

21 in

11 −6 Area of Squares, Rectangles, and Parallelograms

Helpful
Hints

Area of Rectangles =
Length × width

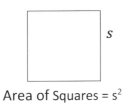

Area of Squares = s^2

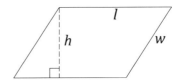

Area of Parallelograms =
length × height

Example:

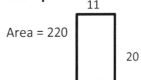

Area = 220

Find the area of each.

1)

22 yd

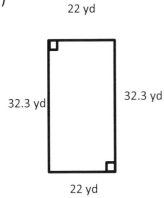

32.3 yd   32.3 yd

22 yd

2)

27mi

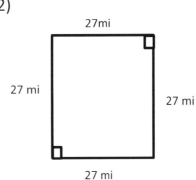

27 mi   27 mi

27 mi

3)

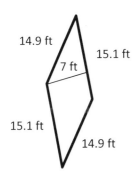

14.9 ft

15.1 ft

7 ft

15.1 ft

14.9 ft

4)

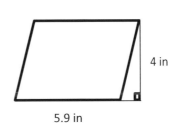

4 in

5.9 in

11 –7 Area of Trapezoids

Helpful $A = \frac{1}{2}h(b_1 + b_2)$

Hints

Example:

A = 252 cm²

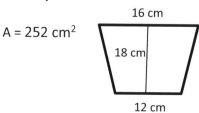

16 cm

18 cm

12 cm

Calculate the area for each trapezoid.

1)

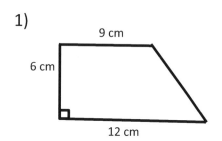

9 cm

6 cm

12 cm

2)

14 m

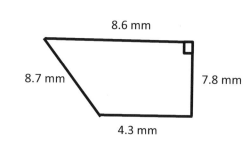

12 m

18 m

3)

22 mi

18 mi

22 mi   3 mi

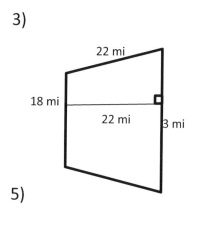

4)

8.6 mm

8.7 mm   7.8 mm

4.3 mm

5)

16 cm

20 cm

12 cm

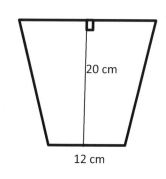

6)

13.5 m

12 m

16.5 m

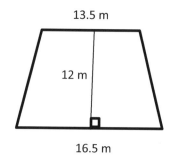

Answers of Worksheets – Chapter 11

11–1 Transformations: Translations, Rotations, and Reflections

1)

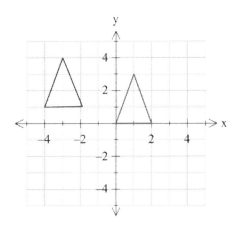

2)

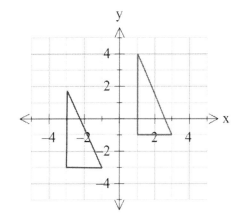

3) rotation 90° counterclockwise about the origin

4) rotation 180° about the origin

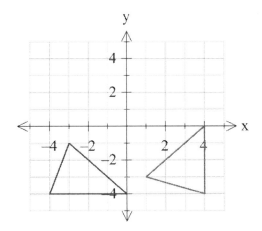

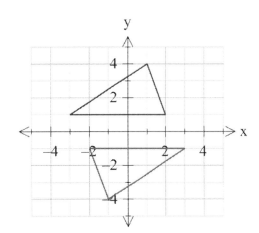

11–2 The Pythagorean Theorem

1) yes   3) yes   5) 26

2) yes   4) 17   6) 13

11–3 Area of Triangles

1) 16.65 mi^2 3) 28m^2

2) 56 m^2 4) 96.8 m^2

11–4 Perimeter of Polygons

1) 30 m   3) 48 ft   5) 35 in

2) 60mm   4) 60 in   6) 40 in

11–5 Area and Circumference of Circles

1) Area: 50.27 in^2, Circumference: 25.12 in

2) Area: $1,017.36 \text{ cm}^2$, Circumference: 113.04 cm

3) Area: 78.5m^2, Circumference: 31.4 m

4) Area: 379.94 cm^2, Circumference: 69.08 cm

5) Area: 200.96 km^2, Circumference: 50.2 km

6) Area: $1,384.74 \text{ km}^2$, Circumference: 131.88 km

11–6 Area of Squares, Rectangles, and Parallelograms

1) 710.6 yd^2 3) 105.7 ft^2

2) 729 mi^2 4) 23.6 in^2

11–7 Area of Trapezoids

1) 63 cm^2 3) 451 mi^2 5) 280 cm^2

2) 192 m^2 4) 50.31 nm^2 6) 180 m^2

Chapter 12: Solid Figures

12 –1 Volume of Cubes and Rectangle Prisms

Helpful

Hints

– Volume is the measure of the amount of space inside of a solid figure, like a cube, ball, cylinder or pyramid.
– Volume of a cube = (one side)^3
– Volume of a rectangle prism: Length × Width × Height

Find the volume of each of the rectangular prisms.

1)
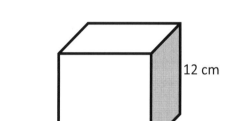
14 cm
12 cm
8 cm

2)
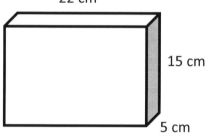
22 cm
15 cm
5 cm

3)
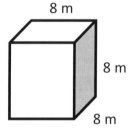
8 m
8 m
8 m

4)
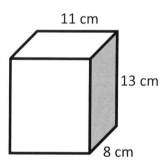
11 cm
13 cm
8 cm

5)
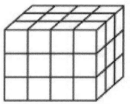

6)
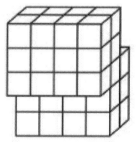

12 −2 Surface Area of Cubes

Helpful

Hints

Surface Area of a cube =

$6 \times$ (one side of the cube)^2

Example:

$6 \times 4^2 = 96m$

4 m

4 m

4 m

Find the surface of each cube.

1)

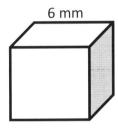

6 mm

2)

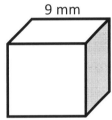

9 mm

3)

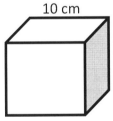

10 cm

4)

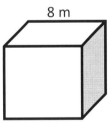

8 m

5)

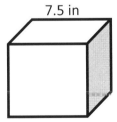

7.5 in

6)

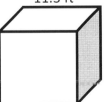

11.3 ft

12 –3 Surface Area of a Prism

Helpful

Hints

Surface Area of a Rectangle Prism Formula:
SA =2 [(width × length) + (height × length) + (width × height)]

Find the surface of each prism.

1)
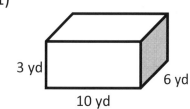
3 yd
6 yd
10 yd

2)
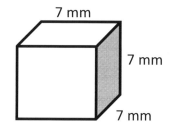
7 mm
7 mm
7 mm

3)
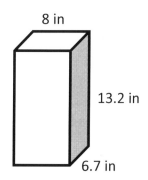
8 in
13.2 in
6.7 in

4)
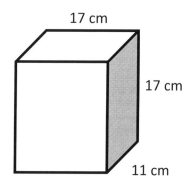
17 cm
17 cm
11 cm

5)
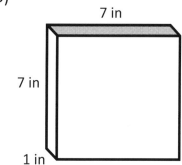
7 in
7 in
1 in

6)
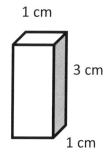
1 cm
3 cm
1 cm

Answers of Worksheets – Chapter 12

12–1 Volume of Cubes and Rectangle Prisms

1) 1344 cm^3
2) 1650 cm^3
3) 512 m^3

4) 1144 cm^3
5) 36
6) 44

12–2 Surface Area of a Cube

1) 216 mm^2
2) 486 mm^2
3) 600 cm^2

4) 384 m^2
5) 337.5 in^2
6) 766.14 ft^2

12–3 Surface Area of a Prism

1) 216 yd^2
2) 294 mm^2
3) 495.28 in^2

4) 1326 cm^2
5) 126 in^2
6) 14 cm^2

Chapter 13: Statistics

13 –1 Mean, Median, Mode, and Range of the Given Data

Helpful

Hints

- Mean: $\dfrac{\text{sum of the data}}{\text{of data entires}}$
- Mode: value in the list that appears most often
- Range: largest value – smallest value

Example:

22, 16, 12, 9, 7, 6, 4, 6

Mean = 10.25

Mod = 6

Range = 18

Write Mean, Median, Mode, and Range of the Given Data.

1) 7, 2, 5, 1, 1, 2

2) 2, 2, 2, 3, 6, 3, 7, 4

3) 9, 4, 3, 1, 7, 9, 4, 6, 4

4) 8, 4, 2, 4, 3, 2, 4, 5

5) 8, 5, 7, 5, 7, 9, 8

6) 5, 1, 4, 4, 9, 2, 9, 2, 5, 1

7) 4, 1, 5, 9, 7, 7, 5, 4, 3, 5

8) 7, 5, 4, 9, 6, 7, 7, 5, 2

9) 2, 5, 5, 6, 2, 4, 7, 6, 4, 9

10) 10, 5, 2, 5, 4, 5, 8, 10

11) 5, 1, 5, 2, 2

12) 2, 3, 5, 9, 6

13 –2 First Quartile, Second Quartile and Third Quartile of the Given Data

Helpful

Hints

Q_1: Splits off the lowest 25% of data from the highest 75%

Q_2: Cuts data set in half

Q_3: Splits off the highest 25% of data from the lowest 75%

Find First Quartile, Second Quartile and Third Quartile of the Given Data.

1) 65, 8, 35, 54, 29, 42, 14, 73, 11

2) 14, 64, 30, 20, 72, 57

3) 99, 37, 83, 62, 74, 49, 59, 40

4) 33, 14, 47, 29, 52, 63, 20, 39, 74, 48

5) 23, 10, 13, 30, 26, 8, 25, 18

6) 35, 60, 20, 80, 95, 15, 40, 85, 75

13 –3 Bar Graph

Helpful

Hints

- A bar graph is a chart or graph that presents categorical data with rectangular bars with heights or lengths proportional to the values that they represent. The bars can be plotted vertically or horizontally.

Graph the given information as a bar graph.

Day	Hot dogs sold
Monday	90
Tuesday	70
Wednesday	30
Thursday	20
Friday	60

13 –4 Box and Whisker Plots

Helpful

Hints

Box–and–whisker plots are a way to display data broken into four quartiles, each with an equal number of data values.

- Q1 – quartile 1, the median of the lower half of the data set
- Q2 – quartile 2, the median of the entire data set
- Q3 – quartile 3, the median of the upper half of the data set
- IQR – interquartile range, the difference from Q3 to Q1
- Extreme Values – the smallest and largest values in a data set

Make box and whisker plots for the given data.

1) 73, 84, 86, 95, 68, 67, 100, 94, 77, 80, 62, 79

2) 11, 17, 22, 18, 23, 2, 3, 16, 21, 7, 8, 15, 5

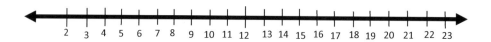

3) 20, 12, 1, 24, 14, 23, 8, 2, 22, 12, 3

13 –5 Stem–And–Leaf Plot

Helpful

Hints

Stem–and–leaf plots are a method for showing the frequency with which certain classes of values occur.
You could make a frequency distribution table or a histogram for the values, or you can use a stem–and–leaf plot.

Make stem ad leaf plots for the given data.

1) 74, 88, 97, 72, 79, 86, 95, 79, 83, 91

Key: 8 / 6 =

Stem | Leaf plot

2) 37, 48, 26, 33, 49, 26, 19, 26, 48

Key: 3 / 7 =

Stem | Leaf plot

3) 58, 41, 42, 67, 54, 65, 65, 54, 69, 53

Key: 6 / 5 –

Stem | Leaf plot

13 –6 The Pie Graph or Circle Graph

Helpful - A Pie Chart is a circular chart divided into sectors, each sector shows the relative size of each value.

Hints

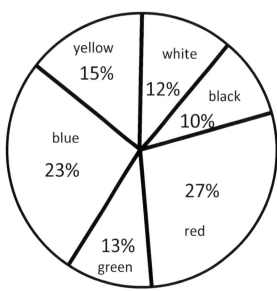

Favorite colors

1) Which color is most?

2) What percentage of pie graph is yellow?

3) Which color is least?

4) What percentage of pie graph is blue?

5) What percentage of pie graph is green?

---

13 –7 Scatter Plots

Helpful

Hints

- A Scatter (XY) Plot has points that show the relationship between two sets of data.
- The horizontal values are usually x and vertical data is y.

Construct a scatter plot.

X	Y
1	20
2	40
3	50
4	60

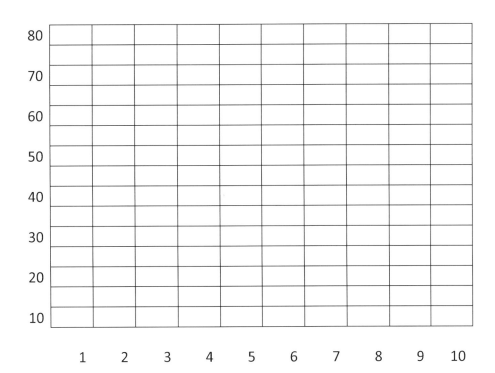

Answers of Worksheets – Chapter 13

13 –1 Mean, Median, Mode, and Range of the Given Data

1) mean: 3, median: 2, mode: 2, range: 6
2) mean: 3.625, median: 3, mode: 2, range: 5
3) mean: 5.22, median: 4, mode: 4, range: 8
4) mean: 4, median: 4, mode: 4, range: 6
5) mean: 7, median: 7, mode: 5, 7, 8, range: 4
6) mean: 4.2, median: 4, mode: 1,2,4,5,9, range: 8
7) mean: 5, median: 5, mode: 5, range: 8
8) mean: 5.78, median: 6, mode: 7, range: 7
9) mean: 5, median: 5, mode: 2, 4, 5, 6, range: 7
10) mean: 6.125, median: 5, mode: 5, range: 8
11) mean: 3, median: 2, mode: 2, 5, range: 4
12) mean: 5, median: 5, mode: none, range: 7

13–2 First Quartile, Second Quartile and Third Quartile of the Given Data

1) First quartile: 12.5, second quartile: 35, third quartile: 59.5
2) First quartile: 20, second quartile: 43.5, third quartile: 64
3) First quartile: 44.5, second quartile: 60.5, third quartile: 78.5
4) First quartile: 29, second quartile: 43, third quartile: 52
5) First quartile: 11.5, second quartile: 20.5, third quartile: 25.5
6) First quartile: 27.5, second quartile: 60, third quartile: 82.5

13–3 Bar Graph

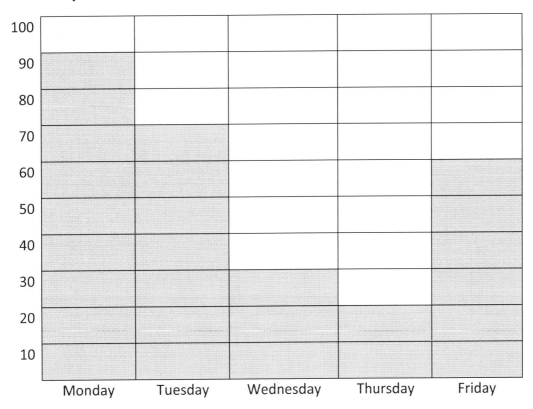

13–4 Box and Whisker Plots

1) 73, 84, 86, 95, 68, 67, 100, 94, 77, 80, 62, 79

Maximum: 100, Minimum: 62, Q_1: 70.5, Q_2: 79.5, Q_3: 90

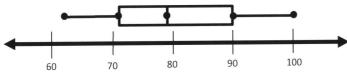

2) 11, 17, 22, 18, 23, 2, 3, 16, 21, 7, 8, 15, 5

Maximum: 23, Minimum: 2, Q_1: 6.5, Q_2: 15.5, Q_3: 19.5

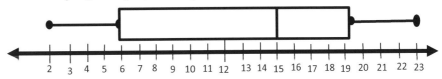

13–5 Stem–And–Leaf Plot

1)

Stem	leaf
7	2 4 9 9
8	3 6 8
9	1 5 7

key: 86

2)

Stem	leaf
1	9
2	6 6 6
3	3 7
4	8 8 9

key:

3)

Stem	leaf
4	1 2
5	3 4 4 8
6	5 5 7 9

key: 65

13–6 The Pie Graph or Circle Graph

1) red

2) 15%

3) black

4) 23%

5) 13%

13–7 Scatter Plots

X	Y
1	20
2	40
3	50
4	60

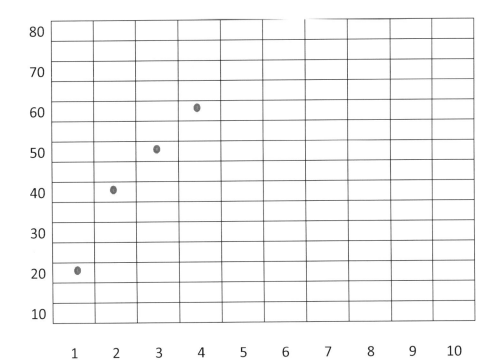

STAAR Practice Test 1

State of Texas Assessments of Academic Readiness

Grade 6

Mathematics

2018 - 2019

1) Anita's trick–or–treat bag contains 12 pieces of chocolate, 18 suckers, 18 pieces of gum, 24 pieces of licorice. If she randomly pulls a piece of candy from her bag, what is the probability of her pulling out a piece of sucker?

A. $\dfrac{1}{3}$

B. $\dfrac{1}{4}$

C. $\dfrac{1}{6}$

D. $\dfrac{1}{12}$

2) In a triangle ABC the measure of angle ACB is 68° and the measure of angle CAB is 52°. What is the measure of angle ABC?

Write your answer in the box below.

3) The perimeter of a rectangular yard is 60 meters. What is its length if its width is 10 meters?

A. 10 meters

B. 18 meters

C. 20 meters

D. 24 meters

4) The average of 6 numbers is 12. The average of 4 of those numbers is 10. What is the average of the other two numbers?

A. 10

B. 12

C. 14

D. 16

5) The ratio of boys and girls in a class is 4:7. If there are 44 students in the class, how many more boys should be enrolled to make the ratio 1:1?

   A. 8

   B. 10

   C. 12

   D. 14

6) Mr. Jones saves $2,500 out of his monthly family income of $55,000. What fractional part of his income does he save?

   A. $\frac{1}{22}$

   B. $\frac{1}{11}$

   C. $\frac{3}{25}$

   D. $\frac{2}{15}$

7) What is the missing term in the given sequence?

   2, 3, 5, 8, 12, 17, 23, ____, 38

   Write your answer in the box below.

8) A football team had $20,000 to spend on supplies. The team spent $14,000 on new balls. New sport shoes cost $120 each. Which of the following inequalities represent how many new shoes the team can purchase.

    A. $120x + 14,000 \leq 20,000$

    B. $120x + 14,000 \geq 20,000$

    C. $14,000x + 120 \leq 20,000$

    D. $14,000x + 12,0 \geq 20,000$

9) Jason needs an 75% average in his writing class to pass. On his first 4 exams, he earned scores of 68%, 72%, 85%, and 90%. What is the minimum score Jason can earn on his fifth and final test to pass?

Write your answer in the box below.

10) What is the value of x in the following equation?

$$x + \frac{1}{6} = \frac{1}{3}$$

    A. 6

    B. $\frac{1}{2}$

    C. $\frac{1}{6}$

    D. $\frac{1}{4}$

11) 12 yards 4 feet and 2 inches equals to how many inches?

    A. 96
    B. 432
    C. 482
    D. 578

12) In a party, 6 soft drinks are required for every 9 guests. If there are 171 guests, how many soft drink is required?

    A. 9
    B. 27
    C. 114
    D. 171

13) Which expression has a value of − 18?

    A. $8 - (- 4) + (-15) \times 2$
    B. $12 + (- 3) \times (- 2)$
    C. $- 6 \times (- 6) \times (- 2) \div (- 4)$
    D. $(- 2) \times (- 7) + 4$

14) What is the value of 5^4 ?

Write your answer in the box below.

15) What is the volume of the following rectangle prism?

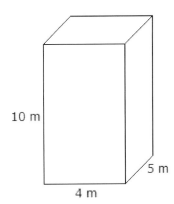

10 m   5 m   4 m

    A. 19 m^3
    B. 40 m^3
    C. 50 m^3
    D. 200 m^3

16) A shirt costing $200 is discounted 15%. Which of the following expressions can be used to find the selling price of the shirt?

    A. $(200)(0.70)$

    B. $(200) - 200(0.30)$

    C. $(200)(0.15) - (200)(0.15)$

    D. $(200)(0.85)$

17) The area of a rectangle is x square feet and its length is 9 feet. Which equation represents y, the width of the rectangle in feet?

    A. $y = \dfrac{x}{9}$

    B. $y = \dfrac{9}{x}$

    C. $y = 9x$

    D. $y = 9 + x$

18) Which expression is equivalent to $38x$?

    A. $(x \times 30) \times 8$

    B. $(x \times 30) + 8$

    C. $(x \times 30) + (x \times 8)$

    D. $(x \times 3) + 8$

19) What is the missing prime factor of number 360?

$360 = 2^3 \times 3^2 \times$ ___

Write your answer in the box below.

20) Which list shows the fractions in order from least to greatest?

$$\frac{2}{3}, \quad \frac{5}{7}, \quad \frac{3}{10}, \quad \frac{1}{2}, \quad \frac{6}{13}$$

A. $\dfrac{2}{3}, \quad \dfrac{5}{7}, \quad \dfrac{3}{10}, \quad \dfrac{1}{2}, \quad \dfrac{6}{13}$

B. $\dfrac{6}{13}, \quad \dfrac{1}{2}, \quad \dfrac{2}{3}, \quad \dfrac{5}{7}, \quad \dfrac{3}{10}$

C. $\dfrac{3}{10}, \quad \dfrac{2}{3}, \quad \dfrac{5}{7}, \quad \dfrac{1}{2}, \quad \dfrac{6}{13}$

D. $\dfrac{3}{10}, \quad \dfrac{6}{13}, \quad \dfrac{1}{2}, \quad \dfrac{2}{3}, \quad \dfrac{5}{7}$

21) Which statement about 5 multiplied by $\frac{2}{3}$ is true?

    A.   The product is between 2 and 3.

    B.   The product is between 3 and 4

    C.   The product is more than $\frac{11}{3}$.

    D.   The product is between $\frac{14}{3}$ and 5.

22)   The average of 13, 15, 20 and x is 18. What is the value of x?

Write your answer in the box below.

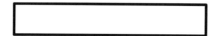

23) Which list shows the fractions listed in order from least to greatest?

$$\frac{1}{6} \quad \frac{1}{8} \quad \frac{1}{3} \quad \frac{1}{10}$$

A.

$\frac{1}{3}$	$\frac{1}{6}$	$\frac{1}{8}$	$\frac{1}{10}$

B.

$\frac{1}{8}$	$\frac{1}{3}$	$\frac{1}{10}$	$\frac{1}{6}$

C.

$\frac{1}{6}$	$\frac{1}{10}$	$\frac{1}{3}$	$\frac{1}{8}$

D.

$\frac{1}{10}$	$\frac{1}{8}$	$\frac{1}{6}$	$\frac{1}{3}$

24) $4 + 8 \times (3) - [8 + 8 \times 5] \div 6 = ?$

Write your answer in the box below.

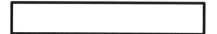

25)   The price of a car was $20,000 in 2014 and $16,000 in 2015. What is the rate of depreciation of the price of the car per year?

    A. 15 %
    B. 20 %
    C. 25 %
    D. 30 %

26)   How many possible outfit combinations come from six shirts, three slacks, and five ties?

Write your answer in the box below.

27) An angle is equal to one fifth of its supplement. What is the measure of that angle?

    A. 20
    B. 30
    C. 45
    D. 60

28) Peter traveled 150 km in 6 hours and Jason traveled 180 km in 4 hours. What is the ratio of the average speed of Peter to average speed of Jason?

    A. 3 : 2
    B. 2 : 3
    C. 5 : 9
    D. 5 : 6

29) In five successive hours, a car travels 40 km, 45 km, 50 km, 35 km and 55 km. In the next five hours, it travels with an average speed of 50 km per hour. Find the total distance the car traveled in 10 hours.

    A. 425 km
    B. 450 km
    C. 475 km
    D. 500 km

30) How long does a 420–miles trip take moving at 50 miles per hour (mph)?

    A. 4 hours
    B. 6 hours and 24 minutes
    C. 8 hours and 24 minutes
    D. 8 hours and 30 minutes

31) If $x = -8$, which equation is true?

    A. $x(2x - 4) = 120$

    B. $8(4 - x) = 96$

    C. $2(4x + 6) = 79$

    D. $6x - 2 = -46$

32) The price of a laptop is decreased by 10% to $360. What is its original price?

    A. 320

    B. 380

    C. 400

    D. 450

33) What is the median of these numbers? 4, 9, 13, 8, 15, 18, 5

    A. 8

    B. 9

    C. 13

    D. 15

34) The radius of the following cylinder is 4 inches and its height is 10 inches. What is the volume of the cylinder?

Write your answer in the box below. (π equals 3.14) (Round your answer to the nearest whole number)

35) A bank is offering 4.5% simple interest on a savings account. If you deposit $8,000, how much interest will you earn in five years?

A. $360

B. $720

C. $1800

D. $3600

36) In a triangle ABC the measure of angle ACB is 75° and the measure of angle CAB is 45°. What is the measure of angle ABC?

Write your answer in the box below.

37) A rope 10 yards long is cut into 4 equal parts. Which expression does NOT equal to the length of each part?

A. $10 \div 4$

B. $\dfrac{10}{4}$

C. $4 \div 10$

D. $4\overline{)10}$

38) There are 60 boys and 90 girls in a class. Of these students, 18 boys and 12 girls write left–handed. What percentage of the students in this class write left–handed?
Write your answer in the box below.

39) Which expression is equivalent to 40 ÷ (4 + x)
   A. 40 ÷ 4 + 40 ÷ x

   B. (4 + x) ÷ 40

   C. (x + 4) + 40

   D. 40 ÷ (x + 4)

40) How is this number written in scientific notation?

0.00002389

   A. 2.389×10^{-5}

   B. 23.89×10^{6}

   C. 0.2389×10^{-4}

   D. 2389×10^{-8}

This is the end of Practice Test 1

STAAR Practice Test 2

State of Texas Assessments of Academic Readiness

Grade 6

Mathematics

2018 - 2019

1) The ratio of boys to girls in a school is 3:4. If there are 350 students in a school, how many boys are in the school.

   Write your answer in the box below.

   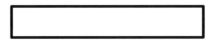

2) 25 is What percent of 20?

   A. 20 %
   B. 25 %
   C. 125 %
   D. 150 %

3) The perimeter of the trapezoid below is 52. What is its area?

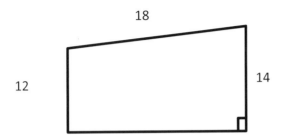

Write your answer in the box below.

4) The area of a circle is 64 π. What is the circumference of the circle?

   A. 8 π
   B. 16 π
   C. 32 π
   D. 64 π

5) A $40 shirt now selling for $28 is discounted by what percent?

   A. 20 %
   B. 30 %
   C. 40 %
   D. 60 %

6) In 1999, the average worker's income increased $2,000 per year starting from $24,000 annual salary. Which equation represents income greater than average? (I = income, x = number of years after 1999)

A. I > 2000 x + 24000

B. I > − 2000 x + 24000

C. I < −2000 x + 24000

D. I < 2000 x − 24000

7) From last year, the price of gasoline has increased from $1.25 per gallon to $1.75 per gallon. The new price is what percent of the original price?

A. 72 %

B. 120 %

C. 140 %

D. 160 %

8) Sophia purchased a sofa for $530.40. The sofa is regularly priced at $624. What was the percent discount Sophia received on the sofa?

A. 12%

B. 15%

C. 20%

D. 25%

9) A bag contains 18 balls: two green, three black, ten blue, a brown, a red and one white. If 17 balls are removed from the bag at random, what is the probability that a brown ball has NOT been removed?

   A. $\dfrac{1}{9}$

   B. $\dfrac{1}{6}$

   C. $\dfrac{1}{18}$

   D. $\dfrac{17}{18}$

10) A rope weighs 800 grams per meter of length. What is the weight in kilograms of 12.2 meters of this rope? (1 kilograms = 1000 grams)

   A. 0.0976

   B. 0.976

   C. 9.76

   D. 9,760

11) $[6 \times (-24) + 8] - (-4) + [4 \times 5] \div 2 = ?$

   Write your answer in the box below.

12) If 40 % of a number is 4, what is the number?

    A. 4
    B. 8
    C. 10
    D. 12

13) Jason is 9 miles ahead of Joe running at 5.5 miles per hour and Joe is running at the speed of 7 miles per hour. How long does it take Joe to catch Jason?

    A. 3 hours
    B. 4 hours
    C. 6 hours
    D. 8 hours

14) 55 students took an exam and 11 of them failed. What percent of the students passed the exam?

    A. 20 %
    B. 40 %
    C. 60 %
    D. 80 %

15) What is the value of 3^6?

Write your answer in the box below.

16) Which of the following graphs represents the compound inequality $-2 \leq 2x - 4 < 8$?

A.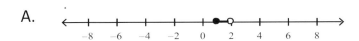

B.

C.

D.

17) The length of a rectangle is 12 inches long and its area is 96 square inches. What is the perimeter of the rectangle?

Write your answer in the box below.

18) The perimeter of the trapezoid below is 36 cm. What is its area?

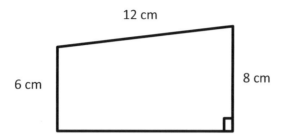

A. 26

B. 42

C. 48

D. 70

19) A card is drawn at random from a standard 52–card deck, what is the probability that the card is of Hearts? (The deck includes 13 of each suit clubs, diamonds, hearts, and spades)

A. $\frac{1}{3}$

B. $\frac{1}{4}$

C. $\frac{1}{6}$

D. $\frac{1}{52}$

20) Which of the following shows the numbers in descending order?

$$\frac{2}{3}, 0.68, 67\%, \frac{4}{5}$$

A. $67\%, 0.68, \frac{2}{3}, \frac{4}{5}$

B. $67\%, 0.68, \frac{4}{5}, \frac{2}{3}$

C. $\frac{4}{5}, 0.68, 67\%, \frac{2}{3}$

D. $\frac{2}{3}, 67\%, 0.68, \frac{4}{5}$

21) How is this number written in scientific notation?

$$0.0050468$$

    A. 5.0468×10^{-3}

    B. 5.0468×10^{3}

    C. 0.50468×10^{-2}

    D. 50468×10^{-7}

22) The mean of 50 test scores was calculated as 88. But, it turned out that one of the scores was misread as 94 but it was 69. What is the mean?

    A. 85

    B. 87

    C. 87.5

    D. 88.5

23) Two dice are thrown simultaneously, what is the probability of getting a sum of 6 or 9?

    A. $\frac{1}{3}$

    B. $\frac{1}{4}$

    C. $\frac{1}{6}$

    D. $\frac{1}{12}$

24) A swimming pool holds 2,000 cubic feet of water. The swimming pool is 25 feet long and 10 feet wide. How deep is the swimming pool?

Write your answer in the box below. (Don't write the measurement)

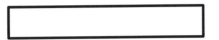

25) Mr. Carlos family are choosing a menu for their reception. They have 3 choices of appetizers, 5 choices of entrees, 4 choices of cake. How many different menu combinations are possible for them to choose?

    A. 12

    B. 32

    C. 60

    D. 120

26) Four one – foot rulers can be split among how many users to leave each with $\frac{1}{6}$ of a ruler?

    A. 4

    B. 6

    C. 12

    D. 24

27) A house floor has a perimeter of 4,221 feet. What is the perimeter of the floor in yards?

Write your answer in the box below.

┌─────────────────────────────┐
│   │
└─────────────────────────────┘

28) The price of a sofa is decreased by 25% to $420. What was its original price?

    A. $480

    B. $520

    C. $560

    D. $600

29) Mr. Jonson spent 44% of his income on rent last month. What fraction of his income did Mr. Jonson spend on rent?

Write your answer in the box below.

┌─────────────────────────┐
│   │
└─────────────────────────┘

30) What is the volume of a cube whose side is 4 cm?

    A. 16 cm^3

    B. 32 cm^3

    C. 36 cm^3

    D. 64 cm^3

31) A bank is offering 3.5% simple interest on a savings account. If you deposit $12,000, how much interest will you earn in two years?

    A. $420

    B. $840

    C. $4200

    D. $8400

32) What is the volume of the cylinder below?

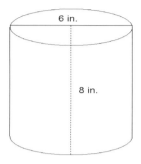

6 in.

8 in.

A. 48π in^2

B. 57π in^2

C. 66π in^2

D. 72π in^2

33) What is the median of these numbers? 2, 27, 28, 19, 67, 44, 35

A. 19

B. 28

C. 44

D. 35

34) What is the equivalent temperature of 104°F in Celsius?

$C = \frac{5}{9}(F - 32)$

   A. 32

   B. 40

   C. 48

   D. 52

35) If 150 % of a number is 75, then what is the 90 % of that number?

   A. 45

   B. 50

   C. 70

   D. 85

36) The average of five numbers is 24. If a sixth number 42 is added, then, what is the new average?

   A. 25

   B. 26

   C. 27

   D. 28

37) What is the volume of a box with the following dimensions?

    Hight = 4 cm   Width = 5 cm   Length = 6 cm

    A. 15 cm^3
    B. 60 cm^3
    C. 90 cm^3
    D. 120 cm^3

38) Last week 24,000 fans attended a football match. This week three times as many bought tickets, but one sixth of them cancelled their tickets. How many are attending this week?

    A. 48,000

    B. 54,000

    C. 60,000

    D. 72,000

39) What is the perimeter of a square that has an area of 169 square inches?

Write your answer in the box below.

                        [   ]

40) What is the missing prime factor of number 180?

$180 = 2^2 \times 3^2 \times$ ___

A. 2

B. 3

C. 5

D. 6

This is the end of Practice Test 2

STAAR Practice Tests Answer keys

STAAR Practice Test 1 Answer Key				STAAR Practice Test 2 Answer Key			
1.	B	**2.**	60	**1.**	150	**2.**	C
3.	C	**4.**	D	**3.**	104	**4.**	B
5.	C	**6.**	A	**5.**	B	**6.**	A
7.	30	**8.**	A	**7.**	C	**8.**	B
9.	60	**10.**	C	**9.**	C	**10.**	C
11.	C	**12.**	C	**11.**	−122	**12.**	C
13.	A	**14.**	625	**13.**	C	**14.**	A
15.	D	**16.**	D	**15.**	729	**16.**	D
17.	A	**18.**	C	**17.**	40 inches	**18.**	D
19.	5	**20.**	D	**19.**	B	**20.**	C
21.	B	**22.**	24	**21.**	A	**22.**	C
23.	D	**24.**	20	**23.**	D	**24.**	8
25.	B	**26.**	90	**25.**	C	**26.**	D
27.	B	**28.**	C	**27.**	1407	**28.**	C
29.	C	**30.**	C	**29.**	11/25	**30.**	D
31.	B	**32.**	C	**31.**	B	**32.**	D
33.	B	**34.**	502	**33.**	B	**34.**	B
35.	C	**36.**	60	**35.**	A	**36.**	C
37.	C	**38.**	20%	**37.**	D	**38.**	C
39.	D	**40.**	A	**39.**	52 inches	**40.**	C

"Effortless Math Education" Publications

Effortless Math authors' team strives to prepare and publish the best quality Mathematics learning resources to make learning Math easier for all. We hope that our publications help you or your student learn Math in an effective way.

We all in Effortless Math wish you good luck and successful studies!

Effortless Math Authors

Made in the USA
Middletown, DE
04 October 2018